Awakening
Consciousness

Awakening
Consciousness

Finding a Larger Version of Self

LINDSAY S GODFREE

BALBOA.
PRESS
A DIVISION OF HAY HOUSE

Scripture taken from the King James Version of the Bible

Balboa Press books may be ordered through booksellers or by contacting:

Balboa Press
A Division of Hay House
1663 Liberty Drive
Bloomington, IN 47403
www.balboapress.com
1 (877) 407-4847

Because of the dynamic nature of the Internet, any web addresses or
links contained in this book may have changed since publication and
may no longer be valid. The views expressed in this work are solely those
of the author and do not necessarily reflect the views of the publisher,
and the publisher hereby disclaims any responsibility for them.

The author of this book does not dispense medical advice or prescribe
the use of any technique as a form of treatment for physical, emotional,
or medical problems without the advice of a physician, either directly
or indirectly. The intent of the author is only to offer information
of a general nature to help you in your quest for emotional and
spiritual well-being. In the event you use any of the information in
this book for yourself, which is your constitutional right, the author
and the publisher assume no responsibility for your actions.

Any people depicted in stock imagery provided by Thinkstock are
models, and such images are being used for illustrative purposes only.
Certain stock imagery © Thinkstock.

Print information available on the last page.

ISBN: 978-1-5043-7507-8 (sc)
ISBN: 978-1-5043-7508-5 (e)

Balboa Press rev. date: 02/27/2017

*This book is dedicated to my six daughters,
Zana, Arwen, Vanessa, Rachel, Faith, and Brianna,
who are the wind beneath my wings.*

*And to my mother Suzanne,
who has always supported my dreams.*

CONTENTS

Why I Wrote This Book..*ix*
Why You Should Read This Book..............................*xiii*

PART I THE SEARCH FOR JOY

1 The Angel 5
2 Learning to Pray 11
3 Facing the Dark Side.. 19
4 Discovering What Really Matters 25
5 Finding Meaning in Life..................................... 37
6 Integrating Your Wholeness 45
7 Healing Yourself, Healing the Earth 57
8 Channeling Grace 71

PART II AWAKENING IN EVERYDAY LIFE

9   We Are One 81
10 Who Else Knows About Awakening?........................... 89
11 How to Know If You Are Awakening 95
12 Water and Energy.. 103
13 How to Be Conscious in an Unconscious World......... 111
14 World Service... 119
15 Conclusions and Insights................................. 125

Afterword... 131
Bibliography of Resources..................................... 133
About the Author 139

Why I Wrote This Book

I've studied spiritual subjects all my life. As a teenager, I wanted to join the Catholic convent or monastery down the street from my home, without thought that I was a Mormon and I heard that the Catholic Church was the "great and powerful church of the devil." I wanted a life of devotion—of communion with Spirit and mystical experiences.

At that time, I even imagined that I could do something to "help save the world" as Jesus did or at least make difference, following the words of Jesus, "Verily, verily, I say unto you, he that believeth on me, the works that I do shall he do also; and greater works than these shall he do; because I go unto my Father" (John 14:12).

Although I've been a seeker, I don't have the accolades that many writers, teachers, and persons of note in spiritual circles have accumulated. I've lost my way many times in my life and have also lost faith in all forms of organized religion. I'm just an average person. Maybe this is what makes my experiences even more relevant.

By grace, I've been touched by Spirit to a peak experience of oneness or an awakening, perhaps because we all are connected and becoming more consciously aware. Unsuspecting people are being touched by a glimpse of oneness, like cells of a big toe that has fallen asleep and is getting its feeling back an inch at a time.

Looking back, I believe my journey began with surrender. At that time, I was deeply depressed—so depressed that it weighed like an anvil on my heart, and I could hardly drag my body through each day. Many parts of my life were working well, but I still couldn't be happy. Even with the antidepressants my doctor prescribed, I couldn't find any reason or wish to carry on with my life. This depression might be termed a *dark night of the soul*. I've discovered many other seekers experiencing a similar path. It's for you that I write this book. I pray that through it, you'll find comfort and direction in my story.

Throughout this time of surrender, I had an experience of seeing divinity everywhere and sought out others having a similar experience. Over time, I found quite a few. It's also for you who resonate with awakening consciousness that I write this book as a reminder that you aren't alone and that many of us are waking up to oneness.

I later discovered there's much more that comes with this awakening experience. For those who are trying to make sense of this epic thing happening through us, I offer some insight and choices. I've learned everything that happens is perfect. There's no need for fear, as you're loved beyond anything you can possibly imagine—and are one with it.

My experience of surrender began when I was brought to my knees both figuratively and literally in deep emotional pain. I screamed at heaven, "I surrender, I give up—you take control. I haven't had any control over my life anyway!" Then I began to listen for guidance and follow the threads of intuition. I asked to know what direction to take. I believe that surrendering to the divinity in ourselves is a key to getting our lives on track.

I asked the universe for meaning in my life, and through some amazing turns of events I realized that I could perhaps give some direction to others, what one of my teachers calls being in the *shepherding consciousness*. I'll be transparent about my pain and my awakening so that you may give yourself permission to have and express your own inner transformation.

What I've ultimately learned is there's no real shortcut to awakening. The process of awakening comes in whatever appears for us in every moment of everyday life—and our ability to be present with it in that moment. It's that simple. This is what our egoic minds try to keep us from knowing. We believe it takes so much work, when in reality we're already perfect just as we are.

There's a path for each person—a path of least resistance set out by our own souls. Your soul knows the way. The only requirements are to accept what is, watch and listen for direction, and know that you are not alone. We're all in this experience together as one. It's through our interaction with life that we become awakened. Relax and enjoy the adventure no matter how it unfolds for you.

It's with great love and appreciation for the *knowing* I've been blessed to experience that I tell this story. My hope is that somehow, in being vulnerable enough to reveal my journey as authentically as I can, all of consciousness may be blessed.

Lindsay S Godfree

Why You Should Read This Book

Many spiritual teachers today say we're at a turning point in Earth's history. They say we're changing our vibration to a "new dimension" or entering the "golden age," the "Age of Aquarius," or the "millennium." Whatever is happening to consciousness on our planet today, we sometimes feel out of control and disoriented. Sometimes life is happening so fast that we feel like we just can't keep up.

This book is meant to be a guide for those awakening to a higher state of consciousness. It will help you understand your experiences. Without some frame of reference these experiences can feel somewhat disorienting. The book will also allow you to have a preview of the exciting times of awakening to oneness that are ahead for all of us.

The information I share is nondenominational and without judgment, criticism, or condemnation of anyone's beliefs. It's written from personal experience and study. I quote scripture not because I'm promoting Christianity but because it offers us a cultural frame of reference that we use here in the West. I believe all teachings are of value. It's up to you to choose the parts of the teachings relevant to you and your life.

In Part I, I offer a reflection of my journey and the steps I took on my path to awakening. Part II presents how you can integrate the steps into everyday life and shares a deeper understanding of my ongoing journey. You'll learn how to align your four lower bodies—the physical, mental, emotional, and spiritual—so that you can be internally consistent with your goals and beliefs, which is the foundation for happiness. I have added exercises called *Food for Thought* throughout this part. You may choose to journal or simply sit in peaceful contemplation of the questions. You'll be offered direction to heal your emotions, step up your energy, and learn to feel better, even joyous. And who doesn't want more joy?

I wrote this book as a sharing of my own awakening so that you may have a better understanding of this experience. Additionally, I share information that I hope will spark a desire to gain more knowledge. It is through the gaining of knowledge that we can design our most meaningful path. All paths lead to awakening in consciousness. Yet our choices allow a long way or a short way, an easy way or a more challenging way, a painful way or one of bliss. Know that whatever is happening is always our shortest path, but it's always within our control to love it or change it.

I AM grateful for another day,
and other opportunity to be my

Higher-Self

PART 1
THE SEARCH FOR JOY

The first part of my journey toward awakening consciousness was a matter of raising my vibrational energy level to a point that would connect me experientially to Source energy. However, I didn't know that at the time. I didn't even know that what I would eventually experience was possible. I only knew I would do *anything* necessary to quit being depressed.

I tackled a plan of action to feel better on every level I could think of. Changing my diet and consulting a doctor. Changing my thought patterns to have better self-empowering thoughts. Clearing my emotions by using forgiveness to make peace with myself. I maintained continual open communication with the universe, looking and listening for daily answers on how to move forward with my life. My pain was a highly motivational force.

To help in the process of gaining knowledge, I participated in a program by Mike Dooley, "Infinite Possibilities: The Art of Changing Your Life," and followed his plan of action for change. I had no idea what I desired in life. I only wanted whatever it took to be happy. I suppose happiness is all anybody wants, and often we spend our time chasing the dreams we believe will grant us that happiness. But as it turns out, happiness is an inside job. It's a journey and not a destination. And there are many habits of belief and behavior that don't serve us in experiencing happiness.

I found myself encouraged to share my stories of overcoming depression with the world. Some teachers say this idea wouldn't have come to me as a desire unless there were someone who needed to hear what I have to say.

Although not convinced that I could be of service to others, if even a few people were helped, it would be worth the effort. Keeping a record would help organize my thoughts and provide clarity to direct myself toward a more fulfilling life.

During this time of self-discovery, I attended an inspiring seminar by Doreen Virtue on how to write a book that was offered by Hay House. To practice my writing and marketing skills, I created the Consciousness Guide blog. I had been working as a travel writer and was looking forward to being a guide to other travelers on a similar spiritual path while I propelled myself toward higher consciousness.

A spiritual awakening can happen in a single moment, or it can develop slowly following years of effort. Regardless, Spirit will eventually lead everyone to oneness consciousness. I look forward to the day when "every knee will bow and every single tongue will confess" the glory of creation (Romans 14:11). Every person will ascend back to the creator of all things; in fact, we're *already* part of the Divine. We only need to wake up to this truth. This is the message I wish to share.

> **"True Oneness with Original Creation is a high level resonance and attractor through which genuine healing and spiritual evolution can take place."**
>
> ~Alex Kochkin

CHAPTER 1

THE ANGEL

I used to have a job driving hospital employees back and forth to their various assigned and remote parking lots. Each night, I drove the shuttle in repetitive circles—eighteen times to be exact—and would meditate on the reason God put me here, in what I considered a dead-end, menial job. I had surrendered to God my job search, and asked the universe to find me the perfect job. This is it?

My astrological guide also had said that this year would be a culmination of the past twelve years, a change of cycles into one of greater consciousness and prosperity. I wondered what that meant to me. My teacher Mike Dooley said to start where you are and do the best you can with what you have. What could I possibly do that would bring value to this kind of job? What God could accomplish through a willing heart in this situation? These were the questions that I meditated upon as I drove.

One evening, I stopped the shuttle to head into the hospital's side entrance for a five-minute break, when a sweet lady stopped me, saying "I'm here for my best friend whose son was brought into the emergency department. He died.

Where do I go to find the main entrance and my friend?" I asked her to wait a minute and let her know I would take her there. But when I returned, she had disappeared into thin air, as though she were a figment of my imagination.

I was deeply moved by the synchronicity and poignancy of what I considered to be a divine meeting that night. I was reminded of the questions I addressed to the universe earlier about the purpose in being in this seemingly dead-end job. I believe everything that happens in life has meaning, and this event had a particularly profound meaning for me. As a result, I knew in my heart I could offer support and direction to others in a nonphysical sense through prayer. And since I most often drove alone for hours, I had plenty of time to devote to this endeavor. There were many souls in that hospital who needed comfort, the presence of angels, and healing. And so I couldn't forget to pray for the souls who had passed on that might also need guidance into the next dimension, to heaven, to God.

I felt somewhat helpless in carrying out this divine work, but it occurred to me that I was in a unique position to pray for many needs, and to pray for those people and souls knowing God would answer my prayers. I believe we all have the power to invoke angels for protection and healing. But then, as usual, there came feelings of inadequacy: who am I that heaven would respond?

I thought of my favorite scripture, which says to ask and we shall receive, and the importance of having faith, believing it's possible to make a difference. Maybe the reason I had this job driving around and around the hospital repeatedly was to build a force field, a grid, an upward spiral of prayer energy.

> And all things, whatsoever ye shall ask
> in prayer, believing, ye shall receive.
>
> MATTHEW 21:22

For every one that asketh receiveth;
and he that seeketh findeth;
and to him that knocketh it shall be opened.

LUKE 11:10

PRAYER AND GUIDANCE

I had not prayed regularly for many years because I was angry with God. I felt he had not answered me, at least not in a way that made any sense to me. Yet my recent new understanding of prayer has allowed me to see that my prayers *are* answered for the highest good for reasons our own souls have agreed to. God knows what he's doing. I now have a return of faith, a knowing that all is as it should be and God is in control. With the belief I'm here for a higher purpose, I accepted my perceived calling to pray daily on behalf of those in need at the hospital.

I had the thought that all I needed to do was some research on the best format for prayer and how prayers should be stated to get the desired results. I would educate myself about what constitutes the most powerful prayers and find some *really* good words to say. There had to be a book with an assortment of prayers calling on God, angels, Jesus, Mother Mary, the universe, and all powers of heaven. On their behalf, I wanted to pray to whomever the patients of the hospital wished me to call upon.

What I wanted was a book that would be a quick fix, with prayers for me to repeat with feeling, with the love in my heart, and belief that heaven would answer. I thought I could just easily buy such a book and be ready to meet the "requirements" of what I felt was my new assignment.

I searched for books online and found none that fit my needs. Then I thought maybe I should just *write* the book I was seeking. I realized I would have to research, compile, and write my own prayers. Prayers I could feel and believe in. Prayers that would meet the needs of those in the hospital. I was determined to help, yet this work had suddenly become a lot more complicated.

The logical progression of my thinking went like this. I need a selection of prayers but can't find a book that speaks to my heart, so I'll have to do all the research and then create one. I like to write, so maybe the book will write itself. Just maybe, by the grace of God and with the help of angels, I'll write a great book.

In my heart, this assignment seemed to be given by the universe as an opportunity to reach out in faith. I once heard we use faith every time we start a sentence without knowing what we'll say to finish it. We don't doubt that once started, there will be a logical end. Several famous authors have said the book they produced "wrote itself." And this is where my book began.

THE NAMES OF GOD

I recently saw a book that listed more than 300 names of God and provided an explanation of where each name originated. More than 300 names! And that didn't include all the hosts of heaven. We commonly hear names such as *the Divine*, *the All Powerful*, *Force*, *Source*, and *Great Spirit*, to name a few. Throughout this book, I chose to use a mixture of some of the names for God that I'm comfortable with. I believe heavenly divine power is meant to be inclusive of all supernatural powers for good, with no discrimination. While you read, I encourage you to use the name or names of God you're comfortable with to receive the book's message and meaning.

There's much dissent about what God should be called. Some names may evoke positive meaning for us, and some may be upsetting and carry negative emotional responses. The word *universe* has become popular when speaking of the All Powerful because it isn't associated with a religion and feels almost scientific. I doubt God really cares what you call him, as long as you *do* call him. He knows what's in your heart.

I believe all names of God carry the same high-frequency energy. Some might even say they're "one with God," as Jesus did. It isn't my intention to embark on a philosophical discussion of theology here. Let's just say we're on the side of goodness and light and proceed from that common ground. Since God is everything, everywhere, there should be a lot of names for God. He is big enough to handle it!

I AM is a name for God. In fact, it was Moses in the Old Testament who spoke to God and was so bold as to ask him his name. God said "I AM that I AM," and in short form God told Moses to say "I AM has sent me to you" (Exodus 3:14).

One of the most important tools for changing your life for the better is to use what are termed *affirmations*. And one of the reasons they work and are so powerful is that they begin with *I AM* as the invocation. Understand that you should be very careful what you declare after saying I AM. To invoke the power of heaven in your life, repeat positive statements every day that represent the person you want to be. God already sees you and knows you in eternal love as that person. Consider how the following affirmations resonate with you:

- I AM kind and loving.
- I AM healthier every day.
- I AM a power for good in everything I do.
- I AM God in action here.
- I AM one with the will of God in my thought and deed.

Food for Thought

When you call 911-HEAVEN in an emergency, whom do you address and who do you think will answer, if anyone? Notice what feeling you have when you see or hear the various names and then ponder that feeling.

CHAPTER 2

LEARNING TO PRAY

As I drove at night, I began to pray the only prayers I knew, as well as fragments of prayers from many different religions. Most often, I prayed that my good intentions were helping others in physical and emotional pain. I felt they shouldn't have to wait for me to get my act together and find the perfect prayer. I would just have to do the best I could. God would answer anyway, right?

I slowly began to realize it wasn't what I said that was most important but that it came from the heart. I do believe words are important and hold certain vibrations and codes, yet I wanted to get to a point where the right words would flow—the best words. But for now, I would have to work with what I knew. Intention itself is very powerful.

JUST DO YOUR BEST

An important principle I've learned is that it's critical to act when the intuition, message, or insight, whatever you want to call it, comes to you. We can all rationalize forever that we're inadequate or we don't know how and might make a mistake. It's equally important to do the best you can with what you have. Part of the joy of the creative process of life is using our ingenuity and the supplies at hand to create a masterpiece. We must start where we are. Where else is there to start?

This process requires that we're honest with ourselves about *where* we are. This may sound easy, but it isn't. It turns out that we're in denial about many things. The process also asks that we be present in the now. As Eckhart Tolle explains it, *the now* is your point of power and the only place you can take action.

I started at a place where I was so depressed and unhappy with life that I could hardly get out of bed in the morning. I was angry, disillusioned, and mad at God. When life sucks, it's easy to blame God for letting a situation happen. When he doesn't seem to help or even hear you (have you experienced that?), how can we keep on believing?

The best I could do at this point was to call to the angels who I felt had always been there for me. I also felt I could talk to the ascended masters of this world. But I was determined to *not* talk to "the Big Guy" himself. I still hadn't resolved my anger that God didn't answer my prayers. I felt unheard and betrayed. I couldn't understand why I didn't have the life I'd prayed for repeatedly.

WHEN IS IT TIME TO CONTACT HEAVEN?

Time magazine published a special edition about heaven, *Discovering Heaven: How Our Ideas About the Afterlife Shape How We Live Today* by Lisa Miller. Surprise! There it was at the checkout station at Walmart, and of course I had to buy it. Heaven seems to be on many people's minds these days and in theaters, too. With the movies *Heaven Is for Real* and *God's Not Dead*, the subject of heaven is mainstream.

With all the chaos around us these days, one might wonder what's happening in our world. Many people are waking up to their connection with God through a change in conscious awareness as what is what's familiar is disintegrating around us. It's the time we've been waiting for—the "last days," "the fullness of times," the "new age," and perhaps the "Second Coming of Christ," or the first one if you're Jewish.

What the *Time* special edition covered was the history of religions and when, where, and who thought up the different ideas of heaven. You may be interested in where your own ideas of heaven come from historically.

Miller states that eighty-five percent of people believe in heaven. She doesn't share what *she* believes but simply states that we all die, and that "We start to die the moment we are born." In conclusion, she points to the idea that any time is a good time to consider what we believe about what comes after this life and why.

Miller also talks about the book *Proof of Heaven* by Eben Alexander. From his work on the brain, Alexander believes science will establish the reality of heaven "in the near future." Won't that be a trip? We can all pray for that. Consider the following affirmation: "I AM proof of the reality of heaven. I see heaven manifest in the world around me. I accept it done on earth as it is in heaven."

Personally, I like the kind of heaven presented in the movie *What Dreams May Come*, one where you create your own reality of heaven, a place that's whatever you dream it to be. I believe we can start creating heaven on earth by *acting* as our higher self, which is one with God, manifests infinite possibilities with our intents, thoughts, actions, and beliefs.

Food for Thought

What do you believe heaven looks like? What can you do today to make your life a little more like the heaven you seek?

The Science of Prayer

Does prayer really work? Although I have a belief it does, it's sometimes hard to demonstrate a traditional practice of prayer, especially when one also believes as I do now that God is within us. It's becoming generally accepted that sending thoughts out to the universe works to materialize energy into form. I look forward to the day the benefits of positive thoughts and speech are common knowledge and science has reached into the formless world. That day is getting closer all the time.

Those who are ill are often highly motivated to turn to heaven for help. As stated in an article by Josh Clark, "According to a study at the University of Rochester, as many as eighty-five percent of people suffering from disease pray in addition to receiving medical treatment. Prayer is the number one supplementary medicine for Americans, more than vitamins, herbs, or therapeutic exercise like yoga." Clark's article goes on to say, "As science investigates connections between the mind and the body, some scientists have found that a person's faith can help him or her live a longer, healthier life. Prayer may lower blood pressure and heart rate, both of which can contribute to a more virile immune system."

It seems that sometimes the higher self "arranges" an illness to prompt one to turn to heaven for answers and discover one's personal connection to the Divine. Many people with cancer or another life-threatening disease have expressed that the time of illness was a growth experience for which they are now grateful. Crisis in our lives requires that we slow down and go within. This going within is where we meet ourselves and discover a larger version of self.

In *Testing Prayer: Science and Healing*, Candy Gunther Brown scientifically approaches the subject of prayer. Here's a snippet from a review of the book: "Dissecting medical records from before and after prayer, surveys of prayer recipients, prospective clinical trials, and multiyear follow-up observations and interviews, [Brown] shows that the widespread *perception* of prayer's healing power has demonstrable social effects, and that in some cases those effects produce improvements in health that can be scientifically verified."

The scriptures say healing is related to the power of faith and energy of love and belief. And it's being scientifically proven that both positive and negative thoughts energetically change the physical world. In the article "Scientific Research of Prayer: Can the Power of Prayer Be Proven," Debra Williams shares research by Bowling Green State University:

> One ninety-eight-year-old woman with pneumonia and congestive heart failure looked upon her illness as God's plan for her. She prayed often for the health and well-being of her family and friends. These attitudes were associated with a serene response to stress and low levels of depression. All signs of well-being that nurture joy in living might even extend one's life. While positive feelings toward a higher power seemed to foster well-being, negative thoughts about a deity had the opposite effect . . . There is cross-cultural evidence that prayer does work. The factors that seem to affect the outcome of these studies are [qualities] of consciousness, like caring, compassion, empathy, and love. When you take these qualities away, the outcome of the study is changed.

Interested in more proof? A review of *When God Talks Back: Understanding the American Evangelical Relationship with God* by T. M. Luhrmann shares that the book is a "remarkable approach to the intersection of religion, psychology, and science, and the effect it has on the daily practices of the faithful." The review goes on to say, "For those who have trained themselves to concentrate on their inner experiences, God is experienced in the brain as an actual social relationship: his voice was identified, and that identification was trusted and regarded as real and interactive."

How incredible is that?

I prayed for change, so I changed my mind.
I prayed for guidance and learned
to trust myself.
I prayed for happiness and realized
I am not my ego.
I prayed for peace and
learned to accept others unconditionally.
I prayed for abundance and
realized my doubt kept it out.
I prayed for wealth and realized
it is my health.
I prayed for a miracle and realized
I am the miracle.
I prayed for a soul mate and realized
I am the One.
I prayed for love and realized

it's always knocking,
but I have to allow it in.

JACKSON KIDDARD

Food for Thought

Where in your life do you believe your prayers have been answered? When has the answer not been what you expected? Was it sometimes better that what you prayed for didn't happen?

Darkness cannot drive out darkness;
only light can do that.
Hate cannot drive out hate;
only love can do that.
- Martin Luther King, Jr.

www.ConsciousnessGuide.com

CHAPTER 3

FACING THE DARK SIDE

As I tried to pick myself up from my depression, I was reminded of Yoda in *Star Wars* as he trains Luke Skywalker in the power of the "Force." He ominously says to Luke as he goes into the black cave of the unknown, "Are you afraid yet? You will be—oh you will be!"

I was feeling afraid, humiliated, and angry about life. I recognized and hated all those feelings. Still I knew that I had to face them—go there, into that darkness. Luke Skywalker met himself in that cave—the dark side of himself.

In contemplation, I asked myself, "What has brought me to this desperate place?" A depression I couldn't shake, a sadness that washed over me like a tidal wave that wouldn't recede and was taking me down for the last time. Even worse, I had much to be thankful for, so I felt guilty and ashamed of my feelings.

As I looked within, I had to admit it: I was angry, *very angry*, at God! Did lightning strike me for saying that? No, I'm I still here. It's difficult to face our darkness and sometimes just as hard to face the light. We avoid talking to God because we are afraid of what he might say.

I felt that life itself had conspired against me to bring me to my knees literally and figuratively, with nowhere else to go but to come to terms with the Divine. I was angry at myself, too, at my higher self—whoever and whatever else had contrived to bring me to this valley of despair and to a talk with God that I didn't want to have.

I hadn't spoken to God for many years, not *really* talked to him, like in a conversation—a conversation where I expected an answer. I said affirmations, understanding that the words *I AM* are another name for God. I sent creative thoughts to the universe with the understanding that the Force would act on my desires and visualizations. But as for God and me, well, we just weren't on speaking terms. What was I to do?

FORGIVENESS

If I were going to move forward with my prayer project, I would have to open the dialogue fully with heaven and all parts of divinity. A new beginning meant to forgive the past, including my anger at the name and personage of God.

Early in my life, I had considered myself to be spiritual and had a good relationship with God. When I followed the rules of my church, it led me to believe I was special. I even felt entitled and believed I was a little bit better than everyone I knew, a little more "enlightened." But that was before life had its way with me, a long time and many crushing blows ago on the road of hard knocks. It was like I had lived a lifetime, or many lifetimes, where nothing seemed to go as it should. *Nothing* seemed to turn out the way it was supposed to.

I was terrified of the feelings of anger and frustration I was holding inside, which kept resurfacing as depression. Feelings related to depression became a familiar state of being, but feeling raw anger was different and so very scary! I asked my sister and my mother to "hold space" for me while I went into the deep well of feelings—to keep myself from drowning. I suggest you find someone you trust to hold space for you if you go through this type of deep emotional pain.

Holding space is about surrounding someone with a lot of love, trusting that as the person is allowed to fully express what happens by feeling the feelings that come up, a deeper healing is at work. Holding space is about allowing experiences and emotions to arise and move through one's energy field. It's about making a safe space so one can feel emotions and see thoughts in potentially profound ways—by not repressing or avoiding the emotions. We carry much less pain in our lives if we can allow the emotions just to be and breathe into them as they're felt and released from the very cells of the body.

I've learned to be more in touch with my emotions. Even though it's still uncomfortable to really feel them, I practice taking deep breaths until I feel better. I now know that our feelings are the guidance system that keeps us moving toward our purpose for experiencing life—that ultimate purpose being joy.

Man is that he might have joy.

BOOK OF MORMON

A very helpful tool for me was a forgiveness worksheet from *Radical Forgiveness* by Colin Tipping. I used it over and over again to forgive myself for my misguided beliefs, mistakes, and wrong choices. I even used it to forgive God. In the worksheet, it says to speak all the words out loud, including what you write. This provides the greatest clearing of stuck emotional energy of the past. I suggest doing such an exercise alone, at a place you can cry or scream or do whatever helps you release the energy held in anger, depression, hatred, shame, and blame.

Food for Thought

In what area of your life would forgiveness provide you more freedom? Are you willing to take that step to rewrite your story into a happier one?

SURRENDER

I know now that the life force, the universe, my higher self, and who I am at any given time are all parts of "God." As stated earlier, the Divine Source has been given hundreds of names as individual personifications, each one a little different. God as the father figure makes it so very personal.

My logical thinking compelled me to realize that if I were part of God, then in actuality I was angry with myself. No wonder I was depressed, right? I was an expert at putting myself down and being angry with myself for so many perceived mistakes. It was my comfort zone, and a familiar mode of operation, to blame myself for everything.

Looking back, I can see that this is the point where I surrendered to the Divine and my own divine plan. This seems to be a common life theme—part of the human experience that we all go through in one way or another. We all come to a point of surrender to what life has given us or taken from us. It's an *opportunity* to submit to a higher power. It's said that people are happier if they believe things happen for a reason.

I believe every one of us must surrender to the Divine within ourselves. Our true, greater version of self. If you don't get the hint by being gently nudged, then life will pull the rug out from under you or hit you with a two-by-four until you get the message.

This push toward awakening may come in the form of illness, the loss of a loved one, a loss of innocence, or a marriage. It may be the loss of a house, job, or even your identity—*anything* that you've mistakenly identified with that *isn't* truly you. You will wake up to who you really are. The real you *is* part of the eternal divine oneness.

I'm now comfortable praying to God and addressing any of the names for divine presence. I realize God is within me. We're all part of the universal oneness of love that is God and will be forever.

Food for Thought

What does being a powerful creator mean to you? How will you choose to create your life consciously?

CHAPTER 4

DISCOVERING WHAT REALLY MATTERS

As I said before, when I surrendered to the Divine, I was at a point where nothing mattered anymore. Nothing seemed important or worthwhile in my life. Many people get to a place where they feel this despair at one time or another—usually after a great loss of some kind. It is here that you connect with consciousness.

I didn't have any reasonable excuse to feel as I did. Mostly, I think my egoic self was just angry that it didn't get what it wanted in life—what I thought I deserved. Now I make transformational decisions to follow divine direction and find real meaning in my life. I would like to share with you some insights I received about what really matters.

One book made a huge impact on me—*The Only Thing That Matters* by Neale Donald Walsch, author of the Conversations with God series. In it, Walsch says ninety-eight percent of people spend ninety-eight percent of their time doing things that don't really matter. Further, he says when all is said and done, we will discover the only thing that really matters is that we find our own connection to Source.

I made the commitment when I had it out with God and read that book that I would spend ninety-eight percent of my time in pursuit of the most important thing to me—the connection to Source. This is what matters to me now since discovering Source is the love that feels like fearlessness and joy. It's the power and energy that flows through and connects all life.

As I pursued a connection to the nonphysical and conducted my own conversations with God, I began to receive more answers. It has come to my attention in my studies that there's a movement in the world of people who are awakening to the awareness of our divine nature. You must be one of these people, as otherwise you wouldn't have been attracted to this book.

It has been said that almost everyone has had a strong spiritual experience of some kind—and most don't want to have one ever again. Maybe it's because they can't find an explanation that makes any sense to them. Any unknown that we can't understand can be very frightening.

It was at this point I realized what I was beginning wasn't just a prayer practice but a journey with the destination unknown. I created the Consciousness Guide, a blog to post about insights that might be helpful to others looking for greater consciousness in their lives. In many ways, it is my journaling practice. In the blog, I provide easy "how-to" steps to those seeking to apply greater mindfulness to everyday activities. Even though we're divine, we're also human beings living in a three-dimensional, physical world. Whether enlightened or not, we're still subject to the limitations of this world and must function within it. Mindfulness is life changing.

It was and still is my intention to document my stories and experiences as I continue to reach for a connection to the Divine. My hope is to give those who are searching for answers some of the explanations and understandings they're seeking. To assist, I provide resources on the blog that are useful when trying to make sense of experiences as the nature of consciousness changes. It will soon become apparent that the whole of our earth is going through a change in consciousness. It's time to wake up. Time to connect with Source.

I can share no greater insight than my own experiential knowing of the reality that we *are* divine.

Food for Thought

What is *your* personal spiritual experience? What *really* matters to you?

STOP BEING A VICTIM

Why be concerned about having more conscious awareness? The most important reason is that with more consciousness, we see the oneness we share with all humanity. We have so much in common with every other person as we take on the different roles each plays in the drama of life. We play out the drama so we can discover how to love and be loved. Armed with this knowledge, it's possible to drop the drama of being either victims or victimizers forever.

All the world's a stage, and all the men and women merely players: they have their exits and their entrances; and one man in his time plays many parts, his acts being seven ages.

WILLIAM SHAKESPEARE

This understanding is a huge shift for mankind and will permanently change the world. So become conscious about your thoughts and emotions to stop the drama of division and your part in it! In doing so, we will experience a whole new existence.

In our life stories, we often feel like victims to the unfairness of life and powerless to defend against the things that happen to us. Or we may feel that to protect ourselves from being the victim in our life situations, we need to become—either consciously or more often subconsciously—the victimizer. Many have concluded that *shit just happens*.

It *is* possible to have more conscious awareness, to step out of the game and exit that revolving door of the victim. It's wonderfully freeing to be conscious of the roles people play (commonly referred to as archetypes). So be aware of the choices you're making each day and decide how you want to react. That decision itself will take you out of the victim stance.

I'll share a personal story that illustrates this point for me. I put my old Suburban up for sale at Christmas because it was my last remaining source for the money I needed to move to another state. I did a visualization of selling the car quickly at my asking price and then sent that intention out into the universe knowing that it would be taken care of. But the truth was that I was terrified of being a victim in the sale of my car.

An interested buyer made an appointment to see the car. I felt that this was going to be my sale. But then a man from out of state called to say he would put down a large deposit on the car if I would take it off the market until after Christmas. He would then come and purchase it at the asking price. It sounded like a scam, but if he were going to give me a large cash deposit, why not take the "sure thing" he assured me it was?

I agonized about this until I was sick. Was I being a victim? He had not even seen the car. I couldn't see a loophole, so I moved forward on the man's deal and the money came in as promised. I promptly used it for my U-Haul and began packing. Still I couldn't shake the feeling that something would go wrong.

The day the buyer came for the car, he abruptly stated that it wasn't what he wanted and asked for his money back. I didn't have the money anymore. But I wanted to be fair to him *and* take care of myself. I didn't want to be a victimizer, but I couldn't afford to be a victim either. What to do? The situation was devastating to me, and I imagine it was upsetting to the buyer, who had a different understanding of our deal.

The car scenario is a great example of how we can get involved in the victim/victimizer dynamic in life situations. I refused to accept the role of either victim or victimizer, and that man and I ended up on friendly terms. I gave his money back in installments as my budget allowed.

The point is that we can choose our reactions and the roles we play even when our thoughts and feelings try to hijack us. By being consciously aware of our decisions, we transcend the experience of playing the role of victim or victimizer. Be awake and aware, and live life consciously!

Archetypes like the victim and victimizer are universal patterns of behavior that once discovered help us better understand ourselves and our place in the world. For more on archetypes, read *Archetypes: Who Are You?* by *New York Times* best-selling author Caroline Myss.

Food for Thought

In what ways do you play the victim in your life? In what ways are you the victimizer? Try to be conscious of the roles that you play.

FINDING YOUR DIRECTION

When we connect with heaven, we may wonder how we'll know the answer when it comes. Be assured—you'll get an answer if you're open to receiving it. Be aware too that your answer may not be what you're expecting. Some people don't want to talk to God because they're afraid of what he might say in answer. But have no fear, as things will always turn out the best way possible for you in the end. Trust.

We all know the fairytale of Hansel and Gretel—two children lost in the woods who leave a breadcrumb trail to find their way home. In one version, the breadcrumbs are eaten by birds, yet there appear shiny stones that glow in the moonlight left by their father to guide them home.

We each have access to a path back to Source and oneness. This fairytale provides us an analogy for life. When lost and unable to find our way out of the proverbial dark forest, the universe leaves us a path to find the way if we look for it. Follow the jewels of truth left for you each step through life's perplexing situations. Your soul knows the way. It's just a matter of remembering.

Send your queries to the universe when looking for and wanting answers. There are clues and answers provided every day. Just frame your question in your mind as clearly as you can, then be expectant for the answer. It speeds the process along when you're *already* grateful for the answer you're seeking.

The answers to your questions sent out to heaven for guidance may come in many ways:

- They many come to you through something another person says or does that will be just what you're looking for.
- The answer might be in a book that you just happen to open to the right page. Many times

when I'm looking for direction, I'll open a book to a random page and find the exact answer I was looking for.

- You may find that the answer will just come into your mind, and you know if you trust your intuition, the answer is correct.
- You may find your answer by writing down a question and then answering it as if you already knew the answer, as if you were counseling yourself.

- You might even be surfing the Internet and come upon the answer you're seeking. Just be sure to check with your inner guidance to discern the truth.

When being open and receptive, you'll be surprised how quickly you will get answers and how clearly the answer comes to your mind. Some refer to this as tapping into the higher mind, and some refer to it as your higher consciousness, intuition, or getting messages from spirit guides or angels.

Whatever you want to call the communications you receive, they will come from deep within you. Daily communication will delight and amaze you if you pay attention. Remember you always have free will to do as you wish. This is *your* life and experience. It's all about making conscious choices. There really is no wrong answer—some paths are just easier than others. See how much easier life flows knowing you have divine direction when you need and want it. Learn to trust yourself.

The answer can't be found in books—
or be solved by bringing it to other people.
Not unless you want to remain a child all your
life. You've got to find the answer inside you—
feel the right thing to do.
Charlie, you've got to learn to trust yourself.

DANIEL KEYES, *FLOWERS FOR ALGERNON*

Food for Thought

What question do you have for God? If *you* were God, how would you answer the question? What if that's the right answer?

WHAT IS CONSCIOUSNESS?

The most profound expression of consciousness is what is also termed the *knower* or the *watcher*. This is the part of you aware of what's going on in your mind but also knows it's separate from that mind.

Why is this important? Because your inner consciousness is your link to all *Consciousness*, which is Source—the great I AM. And it's who and what we really are. The first inkling of this understanding is the day you realize you are *not* your thoughts. A great personal story about this is told by Michael Singer in his book *The Surrender Experiment: My Journey into Life's Perfection.*

I love writing about my journey into consciousness and all the ways I'm finding to explore, become, or reach for a higher consciousness. This is where all life is going in its evolution, ever expanding, becoming even more conscious—the journey of awakening to our divine potential.

It's exciting that we have the ability to look at anything, any part of life, and have a deeper awareness of it! Gaining greater consciousness just requires becoming more focused in any part of your life that you choose to explore, then sending your energy there. Just *living* life leads to greater expansion whether you seek it or not. Isn't that wonderful?

Living life consciously gives it more depth, more meaning, and thus more enjoyment. Speaking of enjoyment, being more conscious of your physical senses creates more sensuality in your life. I love being more aware, seeing more color, feeling more textures, and noticing small sensual experiences like the wind against my skin.

The song "Who Is the Watcher" by Tupelo Kenyon helps animate the concept of becoming aware of the observer within. The use of music and sound vibration is a great way to quickly shift to a higher vibrational level. I recommend listening to the "Music to Feel Better Song Sampler" (see the Resources section).

Recently, the concept of my Self becoming larger than life became more clear for me as defined in the book *Becoming Divinely Human: A Direct Path to Embodied Awakening* by CC Leigh: "Consciousness is the substrata upon which flavor, color, temperature form, etc. all take shape. In addition, Consciousness is that which is aware of the "things" that happen in our experience … Consciousness is the perceiver, and also that which makes perception possible . . . Consciousness, however, is not and can never be an object to be sought, or a goal to be arrived at."

Although we cannot really arrive at
Consciousness by an act of will—
if intention is directed there,
grace will complete the circuit.

THE CONSCIOUSNESS GUIDE

Food for Thought

Are you aware of your thoughts? Do you remember when you became aware that you're *not* your thoughts? What happens when you become more and more conscious of your thoughts and then edit them?

" Simply waking up
to Consciousness,
causes those around
you to follow.
Consciousness is
contagious" ~
Lindsay Godfree

CHAPTER 5

FINDING MEANING IN LIFE

When I discovered purpose in joyously offering my prayers nightly as I drove around the hospital parking lot, I was abruptly promoted to another job elsewhere. I had to ask for divine direction all over again. Change happens a lot! Have you noticed?

If confused about your purpose or direction in life, maybe my story will help. I desperately wanted to live a meaningful life when I was deep in self-doubt and depression, but I couldn't imagine such a life. The choices I had made up to that point seemed all *wrong*.

In my search for meaningful work, I did the basics of asking the universe for a job that would be fulfilling and imagined myself feeling happy at work. I didn't get the jobs that I wanted, so I didn't know what kind of job I would eventually be hired for. I was just in the mode of expectancy. I waited for the answer to my prayer. The first manifestation of my intention was that I was hired for the parking lot shuttle job, and I learned to be happy there. But that was just the catalyst to step up to something better.

My promotion turned out to be working with people who had serious health problems, driving them back and forth from the clinic to the hospital. Just like that, I had a new expanded purpose because now I was more closely working with the people I wanted to help. I focused on helping everyone and doing my job to the best of my ability.

I was rewarded with appreciation and kindness every day. It became the road to happiness that I hoped for but couldn't have foreseen. Heaven provides us whatever we focus our intention on, and I received what I asked for—meaningful work and happiness.

I discovered that service to others is a great cure for feelings of powerlessness. If you find yourself in a career crisis and feel like you've lost direction, consider doing service for others. At least for a while. It will take your mind off your problems, and before you know it you'll be uplifted by your service. Many hospitals and service agencies have a great need for volunteers.

Food for Thought

Where could you offer help to others? Where could *you* be God in action even for just a few hours each week?

TO RECEIVE ABUNDANCE, GIVE GRATITUDE

One thing I felt was lacking in my life was money. We never seem to have enough, right? So my focus on finances became key to learning to live abundantly. As a source of inspiration, I made an online purchase of what I thought was an instructional book, *Simple Abundance: A Daybook of Comfort and Joy* by Sarah Ban Breathnach. I was excited to read it considering its theme of gratitude and abundance, as I needed help in these areas.

Look for abundance by opening the door of gratitude and walking through it.

LINDSAY S GODFREE

Yet shock and disappointment swept over me as I opened the book that arrived in the mail. Except for a preface, some scattered quotes, and blank lines, it was an empty book! I sat in a state of disbelief and confusion, angry at the audacity of the writer and the publisher. In the end, I realized I'd purchased *The Simple Abundance Journal of Gratitude*, and it was not at all what I thought I'd ordered. Having made my requests to the universe, with a state of expectation for help and answers to my current life crisis, I took the time to meditate and pray about the meaning of this event. I asked God, "Why did I receive this empty book?"

After contemplation, choosing to believe the book came to me for a reason, I thought I might as well make the best of it and get my money's worth, so I began to fill it in. I was supposed to write down five things every day I was grateful for, without repeating them, which was difficult in the beginning. The book became a metaphor for my life—empty but filling up. And thus began another chapter in my transformational journey.

As I practiced my daily listing of things I was grateful for, I found it easier and easier to *see* more things that I loved and appreciated. I began to notice the contrast. I previously believed my life was wasted, disappointing, and lacking in all the things I wanted it to be.

As the days of writing down my gratitude turned into a month, I realized I had a new outlook on life. I began to understand that perhaps I hadn't received the abundance I wanted in my life because I wasn't grateful for all the things I *did* have.

One day illumination dawned on me, and I blossomed with an understanding that I *was* rich and didn't even know it. Rich with the beauty of nature, my wonderful family, my opportunities. My job was rewarding as well. I was rich in blessings and had been all the time. I just hadn't seen the blessings and the abundance that was already there. I suddenly realized that even if nothing changed in my life, I *could* be happy. I really understood that money wasn't the road to happiness. Happiness is a choice.

Now I walk around with a smile on my face, thinking "I'm a millionaire and no one even knows it." That thought makes me smile every time.

You too can transition into abundant living by practicing daily gratitude. I am unable to fully explain the differences it will make in your life as you make your gratitude list before you start your day. You simply have to experiment for yourself to receive the full benefit. Reading about it doesn't work. *Taking action* does.

Affirmation

Abundance is all around me and flows to me easily now.

One upgrade to this practice is to be grateful for things before they happen. I was grateful for the kindness of strangers and noticed kindness happening through the day. I was grateful for money from unknown sources. It was exciting to see how the universe would surprise me.

One day a patient left her cell phone on the shuttle. It rang like magic just as I found it under the bus seat. I offered to drive to her hotel to return the phone and was surprised and delighted at the huge reward she gave me. Again, I was grateful!

At one point, I was sure I would win the lottery—I'm still working on that one . . .

Food for Thought

Where can you apply gratitude in your life? Where can you be grateful for opportunities for growth in areas you believe to be problems?

EARTH ANGELS AMONG US

I called on angels daily, and it wasn't long before I saw evidence of them, only not in a way I expected.

The patients I transported were usually seriously ill with cancer or some yet to be diagnosed disease, but they were always kind, smiling, appreciative, and grateful for the help I gave them. I continued to do my gratitude list every morning. I was so grateful for their appreciation of the offerings of my heart while I drove and prayed silently.

My passengers showered me with compliments. One frail little lady I helped down the steps kissed me lovingly on the cheek. In her eyes was pure innocence—a truly angelic look shining through her. Another beautiful example of love named Mary rode my shuttle several times and always called me by name. One day, she arrived for her chemotherapy in a wheelchair. As I situated her on the handicap lift, she spoke of her gratitude for life and how heaven was just not ready for her yet. When we arrived and she was being wheeled away for her treatment, Mary fussed and insisted she had to return to shake my hand. I was so very touched by her loving-kindness. I felt blessed to give her a hug and wished her blessings in return.

When thinking of angels, it's common to envision beautiful ethereal beings with wings. But this type of vision isn't the only case: there are angels walking among us who are real people with mortal bodies. These wonderful people seem to be sent from above and are just what we need at the moment they arrive. We can add them to our gratitude list and feel rich in friends, family, and the kindness of strangers.

Food for Thought

Who are the angels in your life? How have angels and miracles manifested for you?

LIFE PURPOSE

The answer to the following question brings with it a major shift in consciousness—and it may be a monumental belief change for most people. What if we didn't come here to accomplish anything? What if we took form as individualized sparks of consciousness just to feel what that was like? Good, bad, happy, or sad, maybe any experience is worthwhile.

It's well accepted that God is omnipresent and omnipotent and that everything is created from God— the original force. We're part of that creation. We left perfect consciousness as part of the Divine to come here. I wondered if it made sense to be here to try to "do good" in an imperfect world. What if we came here to experience being separate from God and bring that experience, as an individualized consciousness, back to God's presence?

Our purpose for being here may be as simple as to learn how to love. Or perhaps our purpose is to enjoy the adventure of being an individualized spark of divinity in a material three-dimensional world.

Food for Thought

What have you chosen as your purpose? What if your purpose is just to create your own life experience?

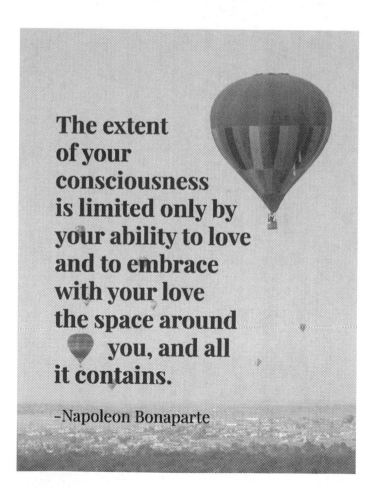

The extent of your consciousness is limited only by your ability to love and to embrace with your love the space around you, and all it contains.

–Napoleon Bonaparte

CHAPTER 6

INTEGRATING YOUR WHOLENESS

Who you really are is so much more than your physical body. You're even more than your four lower bodies, which we will learn about in this chapter. There are many layers in the energy fields that make up our being, and the existence of some of these bodies is not yet known by us.

In well-being and awakening consciousness, a primary concern is the balancing of the four lower bodies. This balancing is an important key to achieving wholeness. The holistic approach. When all our bodies are balanced and in alignment, we're better connected with Source energy and everything is possible. Life flows with ease.

Understanding the relationship of the four lower bodies is important, as they determine how we create our life experience during our time of humanness. Your four lower bodies interpenetrate each other and envelop you, connecting with your seven energy centers, which are also referred to as chakras:

- The *physical* body has the densest energy vibration of life force. It provides the vehicle to interact with matter on the physical plane.
- The *mental* body is the thinking mind. It's the thought process we go through to translate and interpret the world around us.

- The *emotional* body records emotions, reflects desires, and is the tuning fork that directs your path back home to higher planes.
- The *spiritual* or *etheric* body holds the highest-vibrating energies of these bodies. It contains the blueprint of your true self that is one with Divine Source.

Happiness comes from being internally consistent within yourself and in alignment with the four bodies. None of these is the wholeness of you. But as you bring your physical, mental, and emotional parts into alignment with your spiritual body, greater joy, peace, and love flow into your life.

How to Practice Self-Care

As explained earlier, this whole journey began because I was depressed, without energy, and felt like crying all the time. I didn't have the desire to do anything, and I didn't have a clue how to begin to correct my life when I didn't have energy. The logical place to start was with a doctor who could check me for chemical imbalances. Additionally, I realized we can't ask the universe to keep us healthy and happy and then fill ourselves up with toxins and unhealthy foods. We must do our best to help ourselves, right? What follows are suggestions for self-care.

First, take control of the physical. Taking some control of your physical body will give you the basis to then work on your mental body, then your emotional body, and finally your spiritual body. You can work on several things at once if you have strength, but that isn't necessary. Taking control of the physical is a practice where success is measurable. And sticking to a regular regime is the first key to getting control of your life.

The first thing I did was to go on a cleansing diet, rid myself of toxins, and lose some weight under the care of my holistic doctor. I went on a four-week diet: two weeks of the RepairVite program and two more weeks of ClearVite detoxification under the guidance of my health care practitioner; I had used the Fat Flush Diet in the past as well (see the Resources section for more information). I love fruits, vegetables, and protein and now have a vegetable protein smoothie every morning.

There are many detox diets on the market. Choose what works best for you. If you try a regime primarily made up of foods you hate, it will be hard to remain compliant and you'll be setting yourself up for failure, as well as a hit to your self-esteem.

Important Tip

Talk to a doctor about things like hormone imbalance, allergies, and food sensitivities, which might be shaping the way you function in the world.

After the detox, consider a clean food diet. I feel best on a gluten-free, sugar-free, low-carbohydrate diet. Don't forget to do some exercise and drink lots of pure water (see Chapter 12).

Taking care of yourself is critical! Treat yourself as your own best friend. Having a body allows you to do everything important in this physical world. Although we are spiritual beings, we live in a material world. I like to say "Take care of the horse you rode in on."

When you take your daily mind/body/spirit temperature and find you aren't feeling quite right, consider asking yourself the following six questions, remembering not to take *anything* personally or accepting any kind of negativity as your true state of being:

- *Have I had enough water to drink?* This may seem too simple, but not being properly hydrated is the source of more problems than you know. Most people don't drink enough water. Is this something you can fix right now? Get a big glass of water right now and then drink it while reading the rest of the questions. Brain activity requires hydration.

- *Did I get enough rest last night?* Many people are just sleep deprived—there's always so much to do. Taking care of your physical body's needs is your first priority. You can't fulfill your dharma, fulfill your divine plan, or create the life of your dreams without being rested enough to function efficiently.

- *Have I had enough to eat, and was it nourishing?* Some people get so busy throughout their day that they forget to eat and then wonder why they don't feel well mentally or emotionally. It has been suggested that eating small meals throughout the day is the healthiest way to eat.

- *Am I following directions?* Have you been taking your supplements and following the program that your doctor, nutritionist, chiropractor, or your own common sense has laid out for you? Understand that everything you know doesn't do you any good if you don't maintain your commitments.

- *Have I been loving toward myself?* Have compassion for your human condition. It's said that we can only love other people as much as we love ourselves. If you want love in your life, *first* love yourself— not being self-indulgent, but looking out for your needs. Nobody knows what those truly are but you.

- *Have I made a minimum of five daily gratitude entries?* Gratitude changes everything. Offer it daily.

You'll find you're surrounded by abundance and beauty *right now*. In offering gratitude, it will be easy to keep a smile on your face.

One reason I stress the importance of these questions is that, coming from corporate sales jobs and trying to raise six children by myself, I often have found myself putting my needs last. And I bet I'm not the only one.

Food for Thought

What will you do to achieve better self-care? What baby steps can you take today and this week to be mindful of your body?

CHOOSE YOUR THOUGHTS

What you think and feel you bring into form;

where your thought is, there you are, for

you are your consciousness; and what

you meditate upon, you become.

THE ASCENDED MASTER SAINT GERMAIN

To improve our mental health, we must be aware of and responsible for our thoughts. Most people aren't aware of their thoughts, let alone have control over what the mind is saying.

Did you know you can choose your thoughts and just connect to the good ones? Our thoughts filter through an automatic sorting of thousands of associations in the brain.

The brain doesn't decide the right ones to choose—it just selects the most dominant thought pattern. The ultimate freedom is choosing your own thoughts and living life consciously!

Your beliefs become your thoughts,
Your thoughts become your words,
Your words become your actions,
Your actions become your habits,
Your habits become your values,
Your values become your destiny.

MAHATMA GANDHI

We all want the freedom to make our own choices, and that begins with our thoughts. Do you realize how powerful you can be when you *choose* your thoughts? To become conscious, you must take back your own mind first. It's so important to take charge of yourself and take responsibility for your life. This is true self-empowerment. Maybe this idea isn't new to you. But have you put your knowledge into action on a daily basis? If you haven't implemented directing your thought and feeling patterns by conscious choice, then what you know is just a theory.

Outside forces want control of your mind. This isn't a conspiracy theory. Just look at the advertisements that bombard us from every direction. Consider the billions of dollars spent on marketing ploys to sway your thoughts and actions. No wonder many people feel powerless. Take your mind back from the unconscious programming of what others want you to focus on.

Science has shown us how the brain works. When thoughts are repeated continually, they become beliefs and your dominant thought pattern. This thought pattern operates on a habitual automatic track in your mind and runs like a narrative tape as constant chatter. These runaway thoughts trigger—consciously or unconsciously—your feelings and reactions to the circumstances of your life.

When you become aware of your thoughts and feelings, you can choose and then practice new thoughts and behaviors. And with that practice, your new thoughts will become the dominant ones replacing the old patterns in your brain. Before you know it, you'll realize a new and better thought pattern.

You might be surprised what paths your mind wanders down when you're not watching it. When you find a thought that isn't up to your highest standards, replace it with one you prefer—one that feels better.

Here are a few easy ways to change your thoughts, your feelings, and even your beliefs:

- *Write down an affirmation, or several, that you would like to embrace.* Tape the affirmation to your computer, your mirror, or wherever you'll see it regularly. Repeat it over and over again. Change affirmations often so they don't become too routine. For example, "I AM in control of my thoughts, and I choose happiness in my life. Things in my life keep getting better and better." Then continue this thinking to establish the new pattern you've chosen for yourself. Louise Hay is the master of affirmations. Refer to her books at Hay House (www.hayhouse.com).
- *Choose thoughts that simply feel better.* Mentally talk yourself through a series of thoughts or feelings until you arrive at *what* feels better. An example of this method is demonstrated in YouTube videos by authors Jerry and Esther Hicks (see the Resources section).

- *Listen to songs with great lyrics.* The music will repeat in your mind and turn your thoughts to happiness. You can also listen to audio information, which will fill your brain with what you want to think.
- *Direct your attention to whatever you love.* Focus on everything you're grateful for—the people, places, and things creating a happy space for you throughout the day.

In a short time, it will be commonplace to use your God-given free will to create the thoughts, feelings, and beliefs, and ultimately the life, you want for yourself. Being awake is powerful. Live life consciously!

Food for Thought

What thought or feeling did you suddenly become conscious of today? Continue to monitor what goes on in your mind and how it corresponds to feelings in the body.

CHOOSE YOUR BELIEFS

Thinking is the hardest work there is,
which is the probable reason
why so few engage in it.

HENRY FORD (1863-1947)

It's a scientific fact that the thoughts and the beliefs we choose shape our reality in the world. They determine how we see and experience our lives. Many people have come to their beliefs by reproducing the belief system of their parents, their churches, or their peer groups without question, in which case a kind of box has been created for us.

News Flash! These beliefs can be changed. It has been shown through research that with repetition, new pathways of thought are built into the brain and can be deepened into a new belief.

If thoughts and beliefs are a matter of freedom of choice—of free will—then why not choose the ones that feel better? It's a puzzle to me why people choose to focus attention upon and come to believe horrible things. Why not choose the most uplifting and loving interpretation of events you can think of? Why not choose happy, joyful thoughts and the beliefs that support you?

To illustrate, I'll share another personal story. One day, a guest got off my shuttle just as the bells of the hospital were ringing in song. As I helped him out, he smiled and said, "Those bells are ringing for you." Of course, the fact is that the shuttle runs every half hour and the bells ring at that time. I almost always arrive when the bells are ringing. I grinned and thanked him, and then I thought *why not* believe they ring for me?

After that experience, I chose to interpret the ringing of bells as having special significance for me. Doing so would always put a smile on my face. My belief is that this kind man had a significant message for me about the magic of life. It turned the routine experience of ringing bells into an uplifting experience repeated all day long. And it always reminds me that I can choose to believe as I wish.

Life is about *choices*. Choose each thought and feeling with conscious intention. For more instruction on how to choose thoughts and feelings more effectively, consider reading *Infinite Possibilities: The Art of Living Your Dreams* by Mike Dooley.

Food for Thought

What troubling situation in your life could be seen differently? Is there a possible explanation that feels better? Why not choose that one?

The Stories We Tell Ourselves

What we can or cannot do, what we consider possible or impossible, is rarely a function of our true capability. It is more likely a function of our beliefs about who we are.

TONY ROBBINS

The first speech I gave at Toastmasters was titled "Who AM I?" Through personal research, I read that some Buddhist monks meditate on that *one* question their whole lives. It happened that asking that question was indeed transformational for me. I considered long and hard about who I wanted to declare myself to be. At that point, I knew the way I chose to interpret my life and to stand and declare who I am would set the tone for my future experiences. It would be a framework for my own beliefs about who I am and how I would move forward in life from that point.

I searched through my beliefs, through what others have said about me, through the many jobs I've held, and the facts of my life experience. Then I wondered—what tone do I give it? How do I want to spin this story of *me*? It can be told in so many ways from so many points of view.

I continue to work on how I want to tell my story. Redefining ourselves truly is a lifelong process. We may choose to be a different person from one day to the next, from one moment to the next, and life can turn on a dime.

My intention is to inspire you to be aware of your beliefs about who you are and to choose a heroic storyline for yourself. You see, every story can be told in such a way that the glass is either half full or half empty, and both are equally true. It's the same glass. What it really comes down to is that the choice about which way to see it is up to us! Full or empty? Possible or impossible? It's a *choice*. Most choices aren't made consciously but are the reactions of underlying beliefs. We can discover our beliefs by becoming conscious of our thoughts and feelings.

Many of our beliefs have become embedded in our subconscious mind. However, the subconscious mind doesn't determine whether a belief is true or false—it just records what we tell it. These subconscious beliefs determine how we interpret our experiences. The mind looks for—and finds—supporting evidence for the beliefs we already have. The popular motivational speaker Stephen Covey says, "We don't see things as they are; we see them as *we* are." The subconscious mind isn't trying to confuse us. It's just the way the mind works, trying to save us time and energy so we can react fast enough to stay alive.

In reviewing my life, I realize *I am* a powerful creator! I've been able to create according to my beliefs all my life—both the good and bad. My beliefs allowed me to be a financial advisor for American Express, a lay midwife in the home birth movement, the mother of six girls I raised as a single parent working two to three jobs. I also became a long-haul truck driver, a tour guide in Alaska, and a travel writer, just to name a few of the roles in my life. Now I choose to be an author of inspirational books.

Tony Robbins says that what seems possible or impossible for us is most likely a function of our beliefs.

In *Think and Grow Rich*, Napoleon Hill wrote, "Whatever the mind can conceive and believe, it can achieve." I most certainly believe in infinite possibilities. I AM the creator of my life according to my beliefs, and so are you! I look forward to the day all of us realize we're creating our world according to the thoughts we think. Hard or easy? Happy or unhappy? War or peace? Make a conscious choice to choose thoughts that feel *better*.

Be honest with yourself about your story—about who you believe yourself to be. What we think about ourselves is not necessarily true. I encourage you to take stock of what you've achieved and examine what you believe about who you are. It's an amazing process! Adjusting to the stories we tell ourselves is an ongoing adventure. Make it a *great* story—the story you want *your* life to represent. A life lived well.

Food for Thought

How do you want the story of your life to read? How do you want it to end? Consider the ending and work backward to find the things that need to be done next. Take on the beliefs you need to have in place to create this new story of *you*.

CHAPTER 7

HEALING YOURSELF, HEALING THE EARTH

By now you can see that what I thought was going to be a book about prayer has grown into so much more. From the beginning of this journey, I realized some of my depression was physical, and I needed to address it. But the sadness was also a yearning to be who I really am, a larger version of self.

I've discovered that what affects one part of the body also affects all other parts. Imbalance in one of the four lower bodies puts the entire body's energetic system off kilter. I was so tired of my depression that I started improving each part of myself—physical, emotional, mental, and spiritual—in every way possible. Until we are living a balanced life, the whole isn't healed. This is what's called a *holistic* approach to life.

Healing is the order of the day. Healing ourselves and healing the world is needed. All of us are connected energetically. Did you know Earth is seventy-five percent water and so are we? And that our blood has the same pH level as the ocean? The energetics of the microcosm and macrocosm are all connected (to learn more, see the Resources section). Take care of yourself, and the world will be changed for it.

Be the change that you wish
to see in the world.

MAHATMA GANDHI

Whatever our habitual thoughts and feelings are, they may be causing "dis-ease" that manifests in our physical health and in the planetary body as well. Medical intuitives like Carolyn Myss and other energy healers can read energy flow and identify disease in our finer bodies even before it manifests in the physical world. By doing energy work, you can learn to identify in yourself where the energy is blocked, how to clear it, and heal your own life. The book *Chakras and Their Archetypes: Uniting Energy Awareness and Spiritual Growth* by Ambika Wauters provides a lot of information on this topic.

If every day we choose energetic vibrations of anger, hatred, and fear rather than love, joy, and peace, there will be blockages in the flow of our energy. These negatives also slow down the rate of "spin" of our chakra energy centers. The result is stagnation in the flow of energy within us, causing mental density and emotional problems.

You can increase the flow of vital life force—also called *chi* or *prana*—along energy lines called *meridians*. Meridians take vital life force to your organs and cells, healing your brain and your inner bodies as well. The energy blocked in your chakras, or energy centers, will benefit from being cleared by a healer or by energy-moving practices such as meditation, yoga, Tai Chi, and sound therapy.

You are creative in more ways than you ever thought possible. Find a way to locate where your energy is blocked, then unearth ways to get it moving again. Now is the time to discover how to align the energy inside and out, opening the space to step into your power. Too much "heavy" thinking? If so, all you really have to know is to be internally consistent in your thoughts, beliefs, and actions.

SCIENCE AND THE BIOLOGY OF BELIEF

It might help to understand thoughts and beliefs in scientific terms. Did you know there's a link between biology and belief—a scientific vibrational signature that even enters the cells of our bodies? I learned some startling revelations from *The Biology of Belief: Unleashing the Power of Consciousness, Matter and Miracles* by Bruce Lipton. A noted cell biologist and research scientist, Lipton is a voice for the new science called *epigenetics*.

Science has proven that our attitudes, beliefs, and behaviors originate from our observations and interpretations of others early in life. Sometime before the age of seven years, they're hard wired into the brain as synaptic pathways in our subconscious—the mind's "hard drive." Early in childhood development, our consciousness isn't evolved enough to examine the accuracy of the information, much less control the process that turns it into a belief system we don't even know we have.

As we get older, our conscious mind realizes it wants to make some changes to our knee-jerk reactions to life. Most of us have probably discovered that some of our beliefs can work against us in accomplishing our goals and dreams. We may have discovered deep-seated beliefs. For example, we may have a belief that money is the root of all evil and conclude it's good to not desire having lots of money (note that per 1 Timothy 6:10, the *love* of money is to be avoided). We may decide we're ugly or stupid, or the world isn't a safe place and everyone is out to get us. These beliefs fail to help us perform at our best, blocking us from having our best life possible.

As the conscious mind becomes more self-aware, it begins using willpower to force changes in our behavior. But as we exercise the power of will, we find it can get us only so far. In *The Biology of Belief*, Lipton points out that forcing ourselves through the power of will just doesn't work very well. It causes us internal stress and even damages the psyche. He provides case studies showing that the tensions between conscious willpower and subconscious programs can result in serious neurological disorders.

So are we completely stuck with our early brain patterning or plagued with suffering the stress of trying in vain to exert our will? Are we doomed to be victims of our biology? What's a person to do with this information? How are we to change this programming in our brain? Lipton says the answers are in the atoms of our human body. Quantum physicists have discovered that atoms are made up of vortexes of energy that are constantly spinning and vibrating. This includes those atoms and molecules that make up the structure of you and me. Pretty mind-blowing, exciting, leading-edge stuff, right?

By his revolutionary equation $E = mc^2$, Albert Einstein proved energy and matter are the same and interchangeable. Given that information, the answer to human change then becomes one of changing the energy vibration. Changing our energy transforms our beliefs in the subconscious neuropathways of the brain.

Many books have been written about the brain, and many ideas have been presented on the mechanics of changing our thoughts and beliefs. I teach some of these various techniques for change in "Infinite Possibilities: The Art of Changing Your Life" workshops, which are based on the work of Mike Dooley.

In conclusion, Lipton's life of research proved to him that "the Universe is one indivisible, dynamic whole in which energy and matter are so deeply entangled it is impossible to consider them as independent elements." His further study of fractal geometry has led him to believe that to survive, humanity is currently evolving as a biological whole into a state of universal oneness. Fortunately, Lipton predicts a very happy ending for humanity. Every day, there are discoveries in physics and cell research that forge new links between the world of science and spirit—the seen and the unseen—where energy changes our cells and even our genetics. The science of epigenetics sets us up for evolving from a world where survival of the fittest will eventually also mean survival of the most loving.

Food for Thought

What subconscious pattern or belief would you like to change?

EVERYTHING IS ENERGY

Scientific discoveries are proving we're composed of energy. The ideas behind quantum science aren't new. Socrates said that energy, or soul, is separate from matter and the universe is made of energy—pure energy that existed before matter. It's now well accepted that the universe, including everything we know as matter, is made up of energy. When energy is slowed to a denser, thicker vibration, it then is visible to us as matter.

Quantum physics says that as we go deeper and deeper into the workings of the atom, we see that it's made up of energy waves. An atom is an invisible force field that emits waves of electrical energy. Those energy waves can be measured and their effects seen even though they don't appear physically—they appear as vibrational waves. Physicists are now examining "dark matter," which is probably another form of energy in its state of potentiality.

As science explores the depths of matter, it is discovered that when matter is no more, only energy remains. Quanta is both a particle and a wave. It's difficult to comprehend how something could be both a particle and a wave simultaneously, but quanta is both. Sometimes it behaves as a particle, appearing as matter, and sometimes it behaves as a wave, a form of energy. Waves and particles are behaviors of the same quanta. That matter and energy are interchangeable was proven by Einstein.

Atoms are continuously giving off and absorbing light and energy. Every cell in the body has its atoms lined up in such a way that it has a negative and a positive voltage, both inside and outside. Every cell in our body is a miniature battery. Each cell has 1.4 volts of energy, which isn't very much, but when multiplied by the number of cells in the body (50 trillion), it adds up to a total of 700 trillion volts of electricity in the body. The Chinese call it *chi*—the energy used in hands-on energy healing. It can be measured outside the body depending on the sophistication of the instrument used. It's called your *auric field*. As to the question of which has the stronger electromagnetic energy field, the head or the heart, the answer is the heart.

An amazing fact that Lipton refers to in his epigenetics cellular research is that each atom has its own distinct frequency, or vibration. Quantum physicists see that when two atomic waves meet, they either meet in sync, creating a constructive or harmonious effect, or meet out of sync, creating an effect in which they can cancel each other out.

We're all created out of these atomic energy waves, and because it's impossible to separate waves, the new science says what Osho said more than forty years ago—that we're all connected, and our waves are always meeting and getting entangled with each other. Lipton says the result of such invisible energetic exchanges are feelings of good vibes and bad vibes—depending on whether the other energy waves we meet are in or out of sync with our own.

The cells that make up our bodies know what's nourishing and what's toxic to our energy. All animals and plants communicate through vibrations and are affected by sound vibrations when speaking loving or hateful words to them. Water has also been shown to hold energy vibrations, as revealed in the experiments of Masaru Emoto, who wrote *The Hidden Messages in Water*. I write more about the magic of water in Chapter 12.

We've been taught not to be sensitive to our feelings but rather to what people are saying and doing. However, ninety percent of communication is nonverbal. As a species, we're now increasing our ability to sense energy and are becoming more sensitive to it. Meditation is a great way to get in touch with your awareness of energy changes and whether they're nourishing or draining.

The time is just around the corner when a synthesis of science and religion will be achieved and the distance that separates them will simply disappear. As the gaps between matter and energy close, the gaps between science and religion can't exist for long. Matter and consciousness are also one—they're just different manifestations of the same thing. Suddenly, there's no place for duality when energy is all there is. Osho said, "Consciousness asleep is matter, and consciousness awakened is Consciousness. All is Consciousness."

Food for Thought

When are you conscious of the energy in your physical body?

Quick Ways to Raise Your Energy Vibration

What follows are some of my favorite and most beneficial ways to boost vibration:

- *Become conscious of your thoughts.* When you notice a thought that does not serve you, acknowledge it, thank it for showing up, and then dismiss it and turn it into a more pleasing thought. Find a thought that feels better.
- *Find something beautiful around you and feel appreciation.* Beauty surrounds us. Stop rushing. Walk in the grass, smell the flowers, and appreciate your surroundings. Go out into nature frequently.
- *Be conscious of the foods you eat.* Foods vibrate at different frequencies. Consume quality organic produce—food as nature intended it—and feel energetic throughout your body. It will become apparent when food makes you tired, bloated, and sluggish.
- *Drink alkaline water.* Ionized water created with a high-grade machine will contain a high-energy frequency instead of "dead" water. Water in nature is energized as is flows over rocks or by lightning strikes at sea. Water in plastic bottles is toxic and has lost its high frequency energy vibration.
- *Meditate.* Just ten minutes of meditation a day can change your life forever. Think of it as rebooting your system by calming the mind. The subconscious recalibrates even though you aren't aware of it.
- *Be grateful daily.* Making a gratitude list shifts your vibration from focusing on what you don't have to what's already abundant in your life. This single practice is powerful in changing your cellular

vibration. You'll learn to be more aware of your energy vibration and your ability to change it.

- *Listen to uplifting music.* Music is already an energy wave that your body and soul can resonate with. The introduction of certain tonal frequencies will upgrade your vibration and even change your DNA. *The Book of 528: Prosperity Key of Love* by Leonard Horowitz is an excellent resource.

- *Look for good news.* Whether you do an act of kindness for someone or just observe one, it changes your energy and affects your body's chemistry to give you a boost. Resist watching the drama and trauma of mass media.

- *Hug, love, and be compassionate.* Giving someone a hug and showing love and compassion for others will change your frequency for the better.

- *Heal energetically.* Energy healers are available to assist in changing your body's vibration. One tool that can be used is a tuning fork, which can clear your auric field. Electrical current machines can clear your energy. Medical intuitives can find and clear energy blocks to raise your vibration. Work on clearing blockages in whatever ways resonate with you.

- *Spend time with those you want to emulate.* Surrounding yourself with people you admire and want to be like also raises your energy. Join uplifting groups and communities where you feel better from being part of something bigger than yourself.

Ultimately, it all adds up to this: Source isn't outside you but within you. The love vibration you seek blooms within you. It's in your breath and the spaces between the atoms of your body. As you get in touch with the *you* in higher energetic vibrational fields, you'll tap into Source as yourself.

RELEASING NEGATIVE EMOTIONAL ENERGY

Old emotional records from the past are stored in the subconscious and within our cellular memory. As we awaken, those emotions come up to be balanced and cleared—we feel it as pain. We feel emotional pain but may also notice where is it lodged in our body, perhaps as a lump or tightness. It may also show up as disease. It's evidence of the triggering of the pain that occurred when experiencing

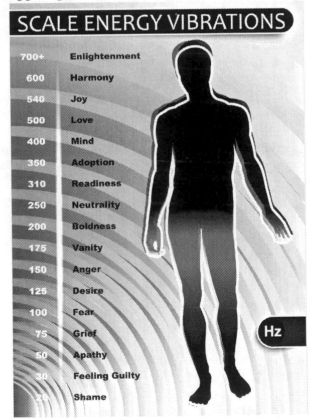

our life events as hurtful. Now we want to release that pain to experience life in a new way.

Our emotions are wonderful because they indicate what's ready to be released. We *want* those emotions to come to the surface. Be grateful for the people in our lives who "push our buttons." They will keep doing that "thing that they do" until a particularly painful memory is released and desensitized so that trigger is no longer active—this is their role in our lives. Eventually, we can chuckle when we notice the personal dynamics in situations that used to trigger us don't ruffle us any longer—we only feel centered and peaceful.

Various tools can be used to release unfavorable energy patterning without repeating those same life experiences. Traditional psychotherapy doesn't seem to work well to truly heal old wounds. It only seems to keep a person in the loop of revisiting and retelling the same sad story. What we seek isn't judgment, vindication, or even justification. What we really seek is transformation and transcendence. Next, I share some of my favorite emotional healing modalities.

Prayer. Prayer and surrender to the Divine works miracles. Don't discount prayer because you may believe it's old-fashioned. Many of us have heard the Serenity Prayer, attributed to Reinhold Neibuhr, yet there's a second part of the prayer that is less well known. I hadn't read this part until I researched the power of prayer, and it has become so very meaningful to me.

Some of you may have negative emotional triggers associated with the Serenity Prayer. Those triggers will allow you to acknowledge the emotions and breathe into them. Some very powerful healing has come from using the prayer. Visit the Resources section for a link to "10 Powerful Prayers for Healing and Change," which may help bring a sense of calm when carrying challenging emotions.

Living one day at a time,
enjoying one moment at a time,
accepting hardship as the
pathway to peace . . .
Trusting that He will make all things right
if I surrender to His will.

EXCERPT FROM THE SERENITY PRAYER

Emotional freedom technique. The emotional freedom technique, or EFT, is also known as tapping. The most well known teacher of tapping is Nick Ortner, and his book *The Tapping Solution: A Revolutionary System for Stress-Free Living* is a fantastic tool. EFT uses light tapping of pressure points while acknowledging the pain and/or negative beliefs you're feeling. Following that activity, you lovingly accept yourself just as you are. This is very healing.

While clearing my pain with EFT, things came up daily that brought tears to my eyes. Sometimes I cried and didn't know why. At those times I would declare, "Even though I'm crying for no reason—I love and accept myself." Initially, it may seem hard to do the tapping or feel silly to say the words. But Ortner and many others have proven that this method works wonders.

Yoga practice. A practice of yoga can locate those memories within the body's tissues that act like trip wires. They let loose in certain poses, resulting in an opening up of the flood gates of unprocessed emotion. The memories may simply be recalled, or the emotional release may be expressed as tears. The key to any of these mind-body communications is to stay present and be open to receiving the messages. Don't pressure yourself. Be patient—remain compassionate with yourself during this release.

Meditation breathing. During meditation, memories often come up with the emotional pain attached to them. It's very healing to breathe into the experience. What does it mean to breathe into the pain? It's acknowledgment of the feelings—just sit with it and be present. Accept and allow it. There's no judgment, no fighting it, no pretending it doesn't exist or pushing it away or burying it inside—just deep breathing. You may feel where the pain is lodged in the body—a knot in your stomach, a tight throat, a discomfort in your heart. Imagine your breath going into that place, and as you breathe out, feel the pain leaving the body.

Emotional processing. Everyone on our planet, regardless of how good his or her childhood may have been, has experienced trauma. We all experience post-traumatic stress to some degree or another. The best way to begin facilitating your own healing is to consciously take care of the child-self present within you. Provide for yourself today whatever you didn't receive in the past from others.

Miranda Macpherson says, "What appears to be in the way—is the way." Emotional blocks need to be cleared to access our potential for love, beauty, and peace. Otherwise, the mind is like a child who falls into the ruts in the road and travels there unable to climb out. Teal Swan uses an eighteen-point process for healing in *The Completion Process: The Practice of Putting Yourself Back Together Again.*

Radical forgiveness. I was in denial that I had anything to forgive, yet I had the intuitive prompting to re-read the book *Radical Forgiveness* by Colin Tipping, which was sitting forgotten on my bookshelf. Using the techniques in it, I could get to the core of my feelings—about work, about authority figures, and about anger at God (as the ultimate authority). The techniques brought up my feelings of not being good enough and of being overwhelmed with life. Worksheets found online allowed me to get in touch with my core feelings and cry them out. Reframing my thinking allowed me to find a new way of being. They offered a perspective that would allow me to be more successful in the life I wanted to live.

Our ego and human mind says "I shouldn't have to suffer." The truth is that often we *do* have to suffer to really change. Like a butterfly fighting out of a cocoon, we must transcend our old self. Understand that sometimes suffering is okay and necessary—like birth.

Our higher self is in control of our lives, and from a higher perspective whatever suffering there is, we've already agreed to allow to happen. It makes us who we are. Ideally, we're grateful for all that life brings. Expressing gratitude is the fastest way for the soul to awaken to consciousness. Know you are a beautiful soul and truly cherished by Life-God-Divinity.

> The wound is the place
> where the Light enters you.

RUMI

Food for Thought

How badly do you want to be conscious? Where in your life has becoming more aware been a painful experience? Can you accept that this pain is okay, just growing pains?

CHAPTER 8

CHANNELING GRACE

Before I began praying for my passengers on the shuttle, *grace* was just a word I associated with other people's churches. Grace was unknown to me. And grace is still largely shrouded in divine mystery—as maybe it should be.

I listened to audio tapes on my hour-long drive to work every day, so I purchased several uplifting audio programs. One that made an impression was titled *Channeling Grace* by Caroline Myss, a noted author and medical intuitive who helps others with her healing insights. I was quite moved by her words.

After listening to her CD, I determined that what the people on my shuttle needed was a good dose of grace. So I decided to do my best to douse them with it whenever they were aboard. Among my prayers then was the request for intercession of grace. Little did I realize that dousing others in grace would rock my world.

My Spiritual Awakening

I didn't know that what I was about to experience was possible—and I really didn't know how to explain it when it happened. I must have had a change of heart—I believe my heart chakra opened in love. What follows is my awakening experience story.

I was simply walking down the lane where I live, as I did daily for months, on the way to my mom's house. Suddenly, I realized I was experiencing being alive in a totally new way. I was in awe of everything. Colors were brighter, and the world seemed to vibrate with life—everything seemed to be multidimensional. I arrived at her house, where I said through grinning, laughing, and a flood of tears, "I see divinity everywhere!"

In a flash, it came to me with a knowing beyond any question that my life was totally perfect. I knew everything that had happened in my life (the one that I previously thought was so awful) was perfect just the way it happened. And if I were killed in the next moment, even that too would be perfect. I had absolutely no fear of anything. This was a huge change, as my normal defensive personality had been so fearful. But now I only felt happiness and peace. It felt so wonderfully light and free to have put all fear aside. I felt loved and loving at the same time.

I walked around in a state of bliss for a week or two. I shook hands with strangers and told them God loved them. I passed out money to the poor I met on the street corner. I cried and was in awe of everything around me. I felt life's conscious energy. I felt a connection with it and to everything that is.

Eventually, I had a thought. "I can't walk around like this for the rest of my life. How am I supposed to function in the world this way?" (acting like a fool smiling, crying, and giving all my money away). I suppose it was the entrance of that doubt and fear that effectively shut down that experience.

I've looked far and wide to find other people who have had a similar awakening experience. The mind wants confirmation and help to define it, label it, understand it, and figure out how to get back to that state. I look forward to be in that knowing feeling again!

Although I've learned a great deal from many people (anyone I can find who writes on this subject), explanations are vague. It seems the terms *spiritual awakening*, *peak experience*, *complete moment*, and *mystical* or *oneness experience* have all been used as possible labels for this type of spiritual event. I've been told as well that such an event will not happen in this way again—it's a door I already went through, and now I'm on my way to the next one. They say that the next one will be just as beautiful, only different.

I would like to say all the things I was *doing* to feel better precipitated my spiritual experience. I'm sure they paved the way to being open to higher consciousness. They increased my energy vibration to a level that broke something open in me. But I must say it was really an act of grace—because as mentioned earlier, I'm just an average person.

This is what makes my experience so wonderful—it proves *anyone* can experience a clear connection to Source. I've read that the seeds of awakening are planted in each person to bloom at pre-established times regardless of the person's spiritual attitudes or beliefs. For me, it was unplanned and unexpected—so blissful and complete and seeming to occur out of the blue.

The main qualities of being one with the larger universal energy field are described by John Beaulieu in his book *Human Tuning*. It may be described as "perfection, completion, effortlessness, playfulness, simplicity, aliveness, and a profound sense of wholeness and well-being . . . The result is a unity between polarities of our internal and external environments, which creates a resonance with a potential of infinite wellness." I would rather describe it as being in tune with infinite possibilities that exist in the field of oneness.

I'm excited to know that *everyone* will change to an awakened sense of self—but everyone will have a different experience of it. Lee Standing Bear Moore says this in the article "What Does a Spiritual Awakening Feel Like?":

> Descriptions are woefully lacking because there are no words that can adequately describe the tremendous euphoria of connecting with the Spirit within. Describing a spiritual Awakening is as difficult to convey in writing as it is to understand the experiences of others because the experience of spiritual Awakening is different for everyone ... a spiritual Awakening is allowing yourself to be open and inviting the living Spirit of God and the love of God to enter your heart. It is the *Moment* when God awakens your soul to a new awareness, a new perception of the world around you. It is the spark that ignites the long-buried ancient spirit within you. An Awakening is when the confused and frightened self transcends to a higher consciousness, an awareness full of love and peace.

I felt the glow of my awakening experience for a long time. I love to relive it in my memory—to connect with that love and peace again. I have the understanding that I AM one with Source energy, and what I experienced is much more real to me than the daily dramas of life. I now have the opportunity to integrate that awakening in my life and anchor it physically into the world with daily practices. I can assist others in their awakening, because in fact there is only One of us here.

"There is no coming to consciousness without pain.

People will do anything no matter how absurd, in order to avoid facing their own Soul.

One does not become enlightened by imagining figures of light, but by making the darkness conscious. ~ CG Jung

PART II

AWAKENING IN EVERYDAY LIFE

Let us embody that light that makes
the darkness conscious.

THE CONSCIOUSNESS GUIDE

After having my spiritual experience, I knew I would never be the same again. It was a true life-changing experience. My new reality was not the perspective of most people I knew. And now I was even more confused about how to relate to the world—something I'd never been very good at considering my introverted personality.

My first thoughts were about finding others with whom I could relate after feeling unity with *all that is*. I wanted to walk among large groups of people and shout, "Is anyone here awake? Please raise your hand so I can see who you are." Seriously! I really wanted to know. I knew I couldn't possibly be the only one feeling this way, but it appeared that no one was talking about it.

I was drawn to an audio book called *The Science of Enlightenment* by Shinzen Young because I thought it would demystify the principles of enlightenment and shed some light on my experience. It turned out to be a book about meditation. After his in-depth explanation of how meditation works, I was so impressed that I started a serious daily meditation practice that I continue to enjoy.

On a bookstore clearance sale table, there was another book I found intriguing, *After the Ecstasy, the Laundry: How the Heart Grows Wise on the Spiritual Path* by Jack Kornfield. In it, Kornfield talks about what life is like after an awakening or enlightenment, which he says are two different experiences. I began to realize that my awakening experience didn't "fix" any of the things I thought were wrong with me. Yet again I was thrown into depression, because from his teaching, a change in consciousness is not enough to totally change one's being—everyone still has "shit" to work out and the emotional body to deal with. I still had to learn to love myself just as I am. This was a blow! I wanted to be magically changed and not have to deal with my "small self." It can be challenging to change fears and give up the protective self, as it takes courage to let it go.

I laugh now about my expectation to reach a destination called *enlightenment* and be done.

I laugh too that I have made things so hard. Stay with me on this journey and learn more about relaxing into God. We are love and happiness, resistance to this is futile.

This part of the book is about the things I learned relative to awakening and enlightenment while trying to understand my experience—and more importantly, to figure out what to do with that understanding. How does it apply to daily life?

"Owning our story can be hard but not nearly as difficult as spending our lives running from it. Embracing our vulnerabilities is risky but not nearly as dangerous as giving up on love and belonging and joy—the experiences that make us the most vulnerable. Only when we are brave enough to explore the darkness will we discover the infinite power of our light." — Brené Brown

www.ConsciousnessGuide.com

CHAPTER 9

WE ARE ONE

Although many people are becoming comfortable with the concept that we are *one*, the deeper meaning of it hasn't quite sunken in, or more accurately, what being one *feels* like. Most people are extremely busy shoring up their sense of self—their sense of duality, of separateness from others, from God, and from the world around them.

We often tend to look for ways to be superior to others yet also feel inferior, which ends up being like a competition. Deep inside, we may feel incomplete, as though something is missing in life yet not knowing exactly what it is. We may have feelings of not being good enough and a sense of loneliness. And we may fear that if we lose our personality or social status and the things that give us our sense of identity, we will cease to be.

The fear of death and the unknown is huge. We've come to this world to experience what it's like to be individualized and separate, so this belief of duality is not wrong—just inaccurate. We're *already* one with all that is. This concept may feel threatening, unstable, and scary at first. But from my experience of merging with oneness, I've learned there's nothing scary or unpleasant about it. It's all love, peace, freedom, and joy.

Oneness

I'm not quite sure at what point the book *Oneness* by Rasha came to me, but it's become my bible, a go-to book when I need comfort. Initially, I needed to read it to connect with oneness every day. It kept me from going into the familiar states of depression and anxiety. I would also do one of five oneness meditations on CD every afternoon to get centered again, because it seemed that by the afternoon I would fall into old patterns of stressing myself out over whatever was going on in my day-to-day experience.

I've underlined much of the *Oneness* book in a rainbow of colored pencils, and I continue to find teachings in it that have taken on new meaning with greater levels of understanding.

You and I are oneness. This is an eternal truth—you are oneness and eternal and cannot cease to be. At some point, you'll eventually wake up to this truth. You can't avoid it. You can't fail in this uniting with consciousness. You *will* find unity. Your only choices are about how you want to get there, how fast you want to get there, and how much pain, disease, and discomfort you want to experience along the way to punctuate your separateness. Resistance is futile and painful. The energy of consciousness keeps rolling in on this planet like waves on the beach with each breath.

We are oneness. All of life is energy. Our energy merges with those around us and with our earth as a whole. You can't hurt anybody or anything without also causing pain to yourself. It can't be done. It's no wonder we feel so upset about the craziness around us! When enough of us wake up to this knowing of oneness, there will be no more war and we'll all most likely be vegetarian. We'll be able to follow the admonition of Jesus, who said "Love your neighbor as yourself" (Mark 12:31). We are our neighbor, and he is us.

The process of awakening is not a "happening" or a goal to be reached—a place we arrive and are done. It's an ongoing process. We often may feel as though we're backsliding or have lost ground in our attainment and understanding. The real attainment of oneness is a state of beingness that we experience over and over again. We can't lose this but only have another opportunity to find oneness at the core of our being again. It's a journey of constant rediscovery.

The opportunity is to *appreciate* this journey. To wake up every day with gratitude for the miracle of life and anticipation of what's next. What miracle of being will unfold today? What part of ourselves will we meet along the way?

How Amazing Are You?

Whereas I used to believe we would lose our sense of self upon dying and merge into "the Force," oneness means that we'll always be an individual spark of consciousness within the whole. We'll always have a record of our life experience from this embodiment and all our others as well. Although I'm okay with the idea of being part of a nebulous force, I must admit I like the idea of being "myself" within the state of oneness much better. We are amazing beings!

Remember how you felt when you learned no two snowflakes are identical? When you realized that each snow crystal is uniquely beautiful in its shape and pattern? Were you awestruck? It blew my mind to try to calculate just how many snowflakes fell every snowstorm, every year, knowing they're infinite in their designs. Just incredible! How amazing are you? You're a more wonderful and unique creation than any snow crystal.

Let's look at a few different ways you're incredibly amazing just by being *yourself*. And if you ever you doubt this, remember the concepts presented next, take a deep breath, and strut your stuff.

Consider the fact that your fingerprints are unique to you, as is snowflake design. One little known fact is that our tongue prints, just like our fingerprints, are unique. And your scent is yours alone, allowing a Bloodhound to track you for miles. Your individual DNA is unique as well and is so complex that it could stretch from the earth to the sun 600 times. If that's not amazing enough, our eyes are also original in design, and their patterns can be used for identity verification.

You're unique not only in physical qualities but also in personality. The science of astrology is calculated by the position of the sun, moon, and each of the planets at the exact time and place of your birth. This calculation of heavenly alignment is based on complex mathematical influences in the solar system.

Numerology is another means of self-discovery through using the date of your birth and numbers associated with your name. Considering that numbers are the essence of all life, delving into numerology can reveal our inner selves, which is yet one more way to uncover your uniqueness.

A science called *personology* measures your facial features and describes your personality by analyzing them. For example, if your lips are full, you're a generous person. If your eyebrows tend to grow together in the middle, you're artistic. It's interesting to see what's written in our features. And it's interesting to imagine how our personal characteristics inside are reflected on the outside.

Palms can also be read, and the latest thing is toe reading. Our uniqueness seems to be written everywhere on our bodies.

Are you beginning to get a sense of how incredible you are? Outside the physical, our own personal way of perceiving the world is unlike that of any other living person. No one has your life experiences—they're yours alone.

Can you appreciate how amazing you are just in terms of your physical and psychological makeup? You're surely as original and beautiful as each crystalline snowflake and more! In truth, the universe cherishes the variation that you and *only* you can bring to life.

The next time you're tempted to feel "less than" someone else, remember how original and uniquely special you are. There's no one in the universe like you. And remember to be the *best* you possible!

We're each infinitely important to God and to each other. I've heard it expressed that our uniquely individual energy vibration is a critical part of the matrix of the wholeness of God. The wholeness of God is like a complex geometrical design. If the point of light and energy that you are would cease to be, the integrity of the whole matrix of all of creation would feel the loss. This is something to think about. What if we're *each* that important?

When you have questions about *who* you are, remember the beauty and originality of the snowflake. How amazing are you? You are infinitely amazing!

Relationship Shifts

We're all just walking each other home.

RAM DASS

While I was having my awakening experience, my oldest daughter, after *forty* years, was making a connection with her father—a father she never met. I was nineteen and he was twenty-nine when I broke my parents' hearts and eloped. Our marriage was annulled six months later when I was five months pregnant and his *other* wife came to get him. That was quite a shock! I never heard from him again.

When my daughter found him through his family, they regaled her with a complete background of his life. It brought up all the pain and hurt of that betrayal and abandonment, but amazingly an understanding, love, and peace also bloomed within me. Perhaps you've faced similar feelings of betrayal by those you've loved and trusted.

I believe that many relationships can be explained by having had "past lifetimes" and that many of our relationships are karmic in nature. Many past relationships and patterns come up in this cycle of awakening consciousness for resolution and clearance. Not being able to recall any of our past lifetimes' relationships, I could only imagine what kind of karma, both mine and his, led to this short-term relationship and a child.

As I meditated on the part he had played in my life, I realized our relationship was based on roles we'd agreed to play for each other in our life dramas. My heart broke for him. We're much older now and have played victim/victimizer roles in many relationships. I imagine the pain he caused himself to give me the opportunity to experience the blessing of true forgiveness is far greater than any damage I received.

Since I was in this place of an open heart of oneness, I wept for him as well as all those who play out parts that cause others pain in life. But what's the purpose of this pain? I believe we experience pain so we can know what victim/victimizer roles feel like and can learn how to love ourselves and each other. It's difficult to play the parts in life that cause others pain. Be compassionate to those whose role it is to be the "villain." Their part in the drama is much harder.

During this time, I was filled with compassion and understanding for all of us in our human condition. In oneness, we interact with other parts of ourselves to experience the emotions of life. As I embraced compassion and understanding for my ex and other men who had broken my heart over the years, I felt a huge energy shift. It seemed like the tumblers of a combination lock had slid into place and the lock was opening. It was as if many lifetimes of discord and hurt suddenly came into alignment—all had become whole. It was an amazing experience!

I'm reminded of the book *The Little Soul and the Sun* by Neale Donald Walsch. In this story, two little souls are getting ready to be born on earth. One soul turns to his best friend and asks how he will learn his lesson in life, saying something like he needs someone to do something terrible so he can learn to forgive. His best friend says, "Oh, I'll do that for you because I love you so much!"

We're all in this grand adventure of co-creating our experiences in a third-dimensional reality. And we have many things in common as we go through the both the trials and tribulations and joys and victories of this experience. As we awaken to our true and divine nature, we can have only compassion for our fellow travelers. I've been blessed to understand and experience this for myself.

My ex-husband and my oldest daughter have now developed a very special relationship. She asked me at one point if he could call, as he wanted to say he's sorry for the hurt he caused me. I assured her that he was totally forgiven—that I had this fabulous clearance of all my past relationships. But she insisted her father needed closure, so I was happy to talk with him and give him that closure.

My point is that we're all in this grand experiential existence together learning love and compassion. All experience is to create a tapestry of beauty and a temple of light. Awakening to consciousness of this larger version of self is where we begin to connect the dots of who we really are.

May your
search
through Nature
lead you to
yourself.
Author Unknown

www.ConsciousnessGuide.com

CHAPTER 10

WHO ELSE KNOWS ABOUT AWAKENING?

Obviously, as much as I wanted to, I couldn't just shout out in public places about conscious awakening or talk about my oneness experience. So it became a treasure hunt to find others who were waking up. I knew I couldn't be the only one having this type of experience.

I decided to search the Internet and follow the clues that Spirit left me to find people who had a similar experience. What I discovered is that there aren't standardized definitions about spiritual awakening experiences. Most people aren't able to put into words what they experienced. And even if they could, those experiences are very personal. It's difficult to expose one's soul openly.

My intention is to open the dialogue about experiences of awakening consciousness by being as transparent as I can about my own.

NONDUALITY

In my search for like-minded others, I first found a group talking about what's called *nonduality*. I'd never heard of this, and it sounded like a double negative to me. Why not just call it *oneness*? To me, the very word *nonduality* points to the opposite—*duality*, which is our illusion of separateness from God.

I ordered several books written on nonduality to see if I could learn more about what had happened to me. *Conversations on Non-Duality: Twenty-Six Awakenings* by Eleanora Gilbert was one of them, and it was comforting to read about the awakening or oneness experiences of others. However, in some of the books, I learned that many of those individuals experiencing an awakening had done so by using drugs, sex, and/or gazing the eyes of another person who had achieved an awakening. Although those modes may be a pathway to awakening, I didn't feel a resonance with any of these groups. I learned that most who achieved an awakening in those ways were unable to maintain a higher consciousness, and what I wanted was to have a feeling of being connected to God and all of life continuously. From all my study of others' experiences, it seems that if we "force" awakenings, we end up still being confronted with the problems of the ego. I think some issues of the personality continue to be present due to not knowing how to integrate spiritual, mental, emotional, and physical aspects of ourselves with God consciousness.

I was searching for a way to be free of my ego patterns that were keeping me from experiencing myself as oneness, or God. The ego, also known as the protective personality, or as Eckhart Tolle calls it, the *pain body*, blocks one from awakening until those magical moments in life when it doesn't.

Relaxing into God

Next in my search, I found a beautiful teacher in Miranda Macpherson (now Holden) and the book *The Journey Home: Discovering the Essential Self*. Miranda had an awakening during meditation in India—a path not familiar to me and my western way of doing things. Still, Miranda was someone I respected and could relate to.

I enrolled in Miranda's webinar course "Relaxing into God," where I had an hour of teaching every week for sixteen weeks. Through her teaching, I became serious about meditation, which is now the one practice that means the most to me in my daily spiritual routine.

For a year, I did an hour-long meditation each morning while listening to *The Supreme Heart of Shiva* CD, which uses the great five-syllable mantra "Om Namah Shivaya" and a series of Oms. I still use this for deep meditation, and I've found that fifteen minutes is sufficient now that I'm used to getting into a meditative state. Many teachers say ten or fifteen minutes of meditation will realign your consciousness and is really all you need.

Miranda teaches the melting of the ego to reveal the authentic self. This is what's meant by *relaxing into God*—the releasing of our need to control life and opening up into a space of allowing. She describes it this way:

> Over the last couple of years, I have been exploring what's practically involved in ego relaxation, letting the unreal melt. I began to map what happened when people sat with me and see if this could translate into a practice that people could access for themselves. This has been coalescing into a method of guiding people into deeper direct experience, and also a series of practices that support us in how to be as we are. Essentially, the practices I have gathered, some drawn from ancient traditions and some have come through as guidance, all support us in:
>
> - opening into what's unfolding,
> - softening our clinging and resisting,

> - allowing grace to unfold without interference,
> - recognizing what has always been here.
>
> This opening, softening, allowing, and recognizing is to be embraced not as a doing project, but as moment-to-moment invitation for surrendering with our whole being, not just the mind. It is a holistic "method" for non-interference.

Although the days of the guru are over and it's up to us to connect with our own power as our divine self, it's helpful to have teachers or mentors provide guidance and direction. I recommend that you find someone to be accountable to who gives you spiritual homework. Consider joining a support group. Becoming involved on a deeper level with others will help you work through fears and mistaken beliefs, which will hold you back from trusting enough to let go and relax into divinity.

UNITY CONSCIOUSNESS

While looking for a community in which to compare my awakening experience, I also discovered the Unity Church. I'm not promoting this church but just pointing out the truth in "seek, and ye shall find" (Matthew 7:7). I was excited to find a group of people of diverse religions and teachings coming together in worship and study. One of the only requirements for being a member of this church is the understanding that God is within us. I never expected to find a large group of people who share that understanding. It was wonderful!

Members at Unity respect my experience and "get it" on the level of God within each of us. All are free within the church community to experience God in any way they choose. Our experience with Source energy appears to be unique, just as we're all unique in our energy patterns. I want to continue to find people to share my experiences with, yet I know that each is still like that snowflake, just a little different and wonderful. Consider finding a spiritual support group where you can experience community.

I've always believed and loved the scriptures that tell us we are gods. I'm excited that I can begin to see the times that are coming soon when we will begin acting "godly." Consciousness is awakening, and part of awakening is knowing yourself as part of God. More accurately, God is *you*.

> Jesus answered them,
> Is it not written in your law,
> I said, Ye are gods?
>
> JOHN 10:34

> I have said, Ye are gods;
> and all of you are children of the most High.
>
> PSALM 82:6

The invitation is to be consciously aware, at the same time, that your individuated spark of the divine oneness is eternal and that you are a necessary cell in the wholeness of all that is.

"Never forget that you are one of a kind. Never forget that if there weren't any need for you in all your uniqueness to be on this earth, you wouldn't be here in the first place.

And never forget, no matter how overwhelming life's challenges and problems seem to be, that one person can make a difference in the world.

In fact, it is always because of one person that all the changes that matter in the world come about. So be that one person." — R. Buckminster Fuller

CHAPTER 11

HOW TO KNOW IF YOU ARE AWAKENING

The energy and consciousness of the world is shifting. And you're aware of it without maybe evening knowing it, as otherwise you wouldn't be reading this book. Congratulations on being perceptive and awake enough to feel the shift! There are many symptoms of awakening. One website listed fifty-one different kinds—some are great fun, some are disorienting, and some are just plain weird.

Awakening may start with a feeling that you're somehow different. You may sense a disquieting, as everything in your life feels altered—that you aren't the self you were before. You've indeed changed energetically. You're much greater than you can possibly imagine, and there are more amazing changes to come.

Some of these symptoms will be subtle and sneak up on you. Some may seem to hit you over the head. Sometimes you may feel as though you're going crazy. I found comfort discovering that others were going through symptoms of increased vibrational frequency like I was. What follows are some common experiences that others have shared on the Internet.

Many people feel a deep yearning for meaning, spiritual connection, and a sense of purpose. You may feel a renewed longing for a meaningful life or have an interest in spirituality for the first time. The material world can't fulfill this longing—a truth I learned that was the basis for much of my depression. My advice is to follow your heart's intuition one step at a time, and the way will open up for you just like it did for me.

Episodes of intense energy might be felt in the body. I've learned that it's a good thing to feel the energy move through me. I enjoy becoming more sensitive to it. Sometimes the energy felt will make you want to leap out of bed and into action. Or sometimes you may experience strange periods of lethargy and fatigue. Fatigue usually follows great shifts of cosmic energy while integrating it into the physical.

What can you do to adjust to what you're feeling? Here are some thoughts. Do your best to flow with the nature of the energy. Resist trying to fight it. Be gentle with yourself. Take naps if tired. Write your novel or journal if too energized to sleep. Take advantage of whatever type of energy you might be experiencing.

As part of awakening, you'll notice that physical manifestation of thoughts and desires is happening faster and more efficiently than before. Be careful to monitor your thoughts and feelings. All thoughts are creative. More than ever, be careful what you ask for. The consciousness level of others will soon become evident by what's manifesting for them as well.

Expect more synchronicity and many small miracles in your life. Synchronistic events tell you you're heading in the right direction and making the correct choices. Honor these clues, as Spirit uses synchronicity to communicate with you. It will seem like you experience miracles every day. If things fail to flow for you, consider a change in direction.

I've experienced that everything contains a message—if we take the time to look for it. Be aware of portents, visions, numbers, and symbols that have spiritual importance to you. Notice how numbers appear synchronistically in your life, especially repeating sequences like 11:11 or 222. I have so much fun "getting the messages" from spiritual reminders and surprises that show up for me daily.

EXTRASENSORY ABILITIES

One of the results of awakening may be a shift to another "dimension," in which case there's an increase in extrasensory ability. All five senses of hearing, sight, touch, smell, and taste increase with an awakening.

New creative talents may surface and become stronger if practiced. Many people have developed artistic talents after an awakening. You may have creativity bursts of receiving images, ideas, music, and other creative inspirations at an overwhelming rate.

Other aspects of an awakening may include strange recurring dreams, hearing voices, seeing auras, new intuitions, and psychic abilities. You may start to have dreams so vivid and real that you wake up confused. You may even have lucid dreams, in which you're in control of the dreaming story. Many dreams may be mystical or carry messages for you.

An increase in intuitive abilities and altered states of consciousness may result in clairvoyance, out-of-body experiences, and other psychic phenomena. There may be channeling of angelic and Christ-consciousness energies. You may experience contact with angels, spirit guides, and other divine entities. Feeling inspiration and "downloading" information can take form as writing, painting, ideas, communications, and dance. Some of my friends have had these inspired downloads.

Others report feeling surrounded by beings or having the sensation of being touched or talked to. Some may feel their body vibrate, which is caused by energetic changes after emotional clearing has taken place. Be patient, and resist being afraid—your body will adjust to this new way of being.

More and more people seem to be experiencing these changes, and it helps to view them as opportunities. You may notice more instant and constant communion with Spirit and will adapt to these new feelings. You're actually thinking and acting in partnership with Spirit most of the time as you go through the awakening process.

LIFE CHANGES: LOSS AND GAIN

Major life changes are triggers to accelerate awakening. As the energy shifts, many people experience it physically as major events that completely alter their lives, such as death, divorce, change in job status, loss of a home, illness, and/or other catastrophes—sometimes even several at once.

At one point in my life, a trigger showed up when my mother needed my help because she was losing her eyesight. I quit my job to be available for her. I was grounded from my traveling lifestyle and totally dependent on her for my finances. It was a difficult adjustment, yet it allowed me time and space for my awakening to take place. I am grateful now that Spirit insisted I wake up.

These forces of change are designed to slow you down, make you simplify, and examine who you are and what your life means to you. Almost everyone will experience forces of change that can't be ignored. Situations occur that precipitate your release from attachments but also awaken your sense of love and compassion.

You'll feel a desire to break free from restrictive patterns, life-draining jobs, consumptive lifestyles, and toxic people or situations. You may feel the desire to be creative and free to be who you really are. You might find yourself drawn to the arts and nature. You may want to unclutter yourself from things and relationships that no longer serve you. The universe is telling you loudly to do it!

Old uncomfortable "stuff" may come up for change and energetic release. The people with whom you need to work out certain behavior patterns that no longer serve you may suddenly show up. Uncompleted issues may arise or situations may occur where you need to work through beliefs surrounding self-worth, abundance, creativity, and addiction.

Thankfully, the resources or people you need to help you move through these issues will begin to appear. Resources appear everywhere with perfect timing to help you on your spiritual journey in the form of people, books, movies, events, animal totems, and spirit guides, among others. These appearances may seem to be negative or positive when you're in polarity thinking (duality). However, from a consciously awakened perspective, you'll see that they're always *perfect*.

You may move through learning and personal issues at a rapid pace. Keep reminding yourself that whatever you need will come to you when a situation or some part of yourself is ready to be healed. Welcome what appear to be challenges with love, courage, and patience no matter what comes up, and you'll move through the issues quickly and with less suffering.

A sense of oneness with all in life may also occur, like it did for me, including feelings of being closer to animals and plants, some of which may even have messages for you. Additionally, you may have a direct experience of wholeness and transcendent awareness—being flooded with love for all life. Compassionate detachment or unconditional love for all is what lifts us up to higher levels of consciousness and joy. You may experience moments of joy and bliss and a deep sense of peace, knowing that you're never alone.

Physical Symptoms

And finally, there are likely to be the physical symptoms, which can include headaches, backaches, neck pains, signs of flu, digestive problems, muscular spasms or cramps, racing heartbeat, chest pains, changes in sexual desire, numbness or pain in the limbs, and involuntary vocalizations or bodily movements. Quite an assortment!

My experience with these symptoms is that they come and go. I went to a primary care doctor and an endocrinologist to discover what I can do to help this process along on a physical level. I also changed my diet to be gluten- and sugar free for a time. I'm attentive to taking my vitamin supplements and drinking a protein shake and lots of alkaline water daily.

Remember to seek medical and/or dietary help if you need it. Once you've determined that what's happening is *not* a medical condition that should be taken care of by drugs, supplements, or naturopathic means, relax in the realization that it's only temporary—it will pass. What follows are some other physical experiences you may have as your energy shifts around the time of awakening.

Changes in eating habits often surface, and you may have strange cravings, food intolerances, or allergies you never had before. Your body will tell you what it can no longer tolerate as you change to a new frequency. You might also be cleansing yourself of toxins now. As you grow spiritually, you become more sensitive to everything around you, including toxins and food combinations. I found that I can't drink alcohol anymore without unfavorable consequences.

Dizziness or light-headedness may occur when clearing a big emotional issue and your body is adjusting to a "lighter" state. Anchor yourself by eating protein. Sometimes it feels right to eat comfort foods. Resist judging food to be right or wrong for you—just trust your inner guidance to know what you need at any given moment. It helps to take your shoes off and connect to the earth—put your feet in the green grass for a few minutes. In addition, drink a lot of water during this time to stay hydrated. You'll read more about water and energy in Chapter 12.

You may experience changing sleep patterns, restlessness, and hot feet, and you may feel tingling, itching, prickly, crawling sensations along the scalp and/or down the spine—this is energy activation at the crown of the head.

You may notice emotional and mental confusion. You may have feelings that you need to get your life straightened out, as it may feel like a disorganized mess. At the same time, you may have issues with retaining focus. There's a perception that time is accelerating because you've had so many changes introduced into your life at once.

Brain fog can show up in your capacity for order, organization, structure, linear sequencing, analysis, evaluation, precision, focus, problem solving, and mathematics. As a result, you may have memory lapses, place words in the wrong sequence, be unable or lack desire to read for very long, note an inability to focus, forget what you're just about to say, and experience feelings of confusion and/or being scattered. When these symptoms occur during awakening, resist worry. It's the result of increased psychic abilities, intuitive knowing, feelings, and compassion.

A racing heart or heart palpitations usually accompany your heart "opening." This may last for only a few moments and indicate that the heart is balancing itself after an emotional release. Resist a sense of panic even though the experience may be terrifying. Most likely, nothing is wrong with your heart. However, be sure to get medical attention when needed. Consult your doctor about any conditions that cause you concern.

I once experienced a very painful feeling of fear in every cell of my body. I could hardly stand still with the pain in my limbs. I had no reason to be fearful; it was just emotional residue in my body that needed to be released. Many days, I've needed more sleep to process the energy and must slow down and rest.

As a perk, you may look younger and have more energy while awakening. Hooray! When clearing emotional issues and releasing limiting beliefs of heavy baggage from the past, you *do* feel lighter. Your frequency is higher. You love yourself and life more. You begin to resemble the perfect you—who you *really* are. Not all symptoms are unpleasant.

The symptoms mentioned may occur before and/or after an awakening experience. You may also notice change in small increments and one day see life from a whole new perspective of oneness with all life while not feeling many symptoms. No matter how you receive the energetic changes, remember everything is perfect just the way it is!

CHAPTER 12

WATER AND ENERGY

I would like to explain something very practical that's critical to your physical well-being. We can't have true health within, or operate at our potential, if the physical body is not well. Additionally, mental, emotional, and spiritual health depends on proper hydration of the body.

Our bodies are seventy-five percent water, and every cell needs water to work properly. The brain is eighty-five percent water and is the first organ to suffer when we're dehydrated. We begin to have brain fog and memory loss without water—the biological conductor of energy. Neuronal pathways need hydration to keep firing.

Here are two interesting facts: the earth is also seventy-five percent water, and the pH of that water is the same as our bodies. Yet another sign that we are one with Mother Earth.

When I consulted with Dr. Sue Morter about what kind of diet would help in the awakening process, she said "an alkaline one." Alkaline means that pH is negative. The body is always trying to maintain equilibrium at a pH of 7.365, which is slightly alkaline. Ionized water helps keep the body at its optimum slightly alkaline state. Ionizing also gives the water a negative energy charge.

I believe that hydrating with alkaline water allows the body to achieve and hold a higher energy vibration that's part of increasing consciousness. The restructuring of the water molecule by a high-powered ionizer not only allows water to better penetrate the cellular walls but also increases its ability to hold the spiritual energy referred to as "light."

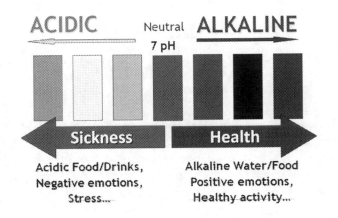

WATER ISN'T JUST WATER

Water. We live on a planet that's full of it. It's even called the *blue planet* because of all the water here. Many of us take it for granted. Others have learned to carry a water bottle with them for health reasons. Yet all of us expect to have access to clean water.

If you haven't studied water, you might think "water is just water." But we can't totally appreciate what a miracle water really is. We may tend to believe that as long as drinking water is available, it doesn't really matter what kind it is or what's in it. What about being conscious of the quality of the water we drink—isn't that important?

I want to share a few important things about one of my new passions—*water*. Let's briefly look at what's in tap water, what's in bottled water, and an alternative source to keep our bodies hydrated and healthy.

As stated earlier, our bodies are composed of about seventy-five percent water. Everything that happens in our bodies happens in water. Our thoughts even happen in water. It takes water to transmit information, and the electrical energy from cell to cell happens in water. Our blood is mostly water. Even our body's waste system is mostly water. There are hundreds of symptoms attributed to dehydration, including death! What follows are some commonly asked questions.

How much water do we need to drink? Everyone has probably heard the rule that a person should drink eight glasses of water a day (eight ounces each). The Mayo Clinic website states the amount is probably more than that and requirements vary depending on activity level, gender, and other factors. Our bodies lose about ten cups just sitting around breathing. And even with all the information about hydration, you might discover, like I did, that you're just not drinking enough water. A healthy amount turns out to be about a gallon a day. I don't know about you, but drinking that much water is likened to a chore. Water just doesn't taste good to me, especially tap water, and who knows what kind of chemicals they put into it to make it "safe" to drink.

What about drinking fun, flavorful, fizzy soda? What happens to our children and grandchildren who love drinking soda? Not only are they having problems with obesity and diabetes, but they're increasingly at risk of cancer. I could talk for a long time on the dangers of drinking soda. In an article from *AARP The Magazine*, it is stated that the number one thing to do to avoid cancer is to stop drinking soda, as one study cited shows that people who drink two or more sugar-sweetened soft drinks a week are eighty-seven percent more likely to get cancer. Diet drinks are found to be even worse culprits.

How about drinking bottled water? Most people today are drinking bottled water. Here's a startling fact—more money is spent on bottled water in this country than on gasoline, and we're always complaining about how much we spend on gas. Number five on the AARP article's list of things to do to avoid cancer is *ban the bottle*, which states "one study found that about a third of bottled water brands contained bacterial or chemical contaminants, including carcinogens in levels exceeding state or industry standards," primarily because of the plastic.

Plastic bottles aren't great for the environment either— they don't deteriorate and aren't biodegradable. Many diseases will never be cured until the toxins found in plastics are out of our bodies. And currently, there are large plastic dumps in our oceans with no place to go, which is a crime.

Apparently, there are no standards for the water itself in bottled water products. It could be tap water, or it could be denatured water, which is not accessible to your cells for hydration. We really don't know what we're drinking when drinking bottled water.

What's a body to do? Thank goodness there's another option—alkaline, ionized, antioxidant, restructured water. Not only does it quickly hydrate the cells, it also provides antioxidants that defend against cancer-causing free radicals in the body. The technology comes from Japan and is popular all over the world, yet it has only recently been introduced in the United States.

This is water you make fresh with a state-of-the-art water filter, and this revolutionary in-home alkaline water ionization technology is the best there is. It's convenient, and you can have peace of mind about your health while drinking it. And it tastes good!

How Ionized Water Can Help You

We all know we should drink more water. I've shared some huge and important differences in drinking water, and now you know that all drinking water is *not* created equally.

How can ionized water help you? There are three quick ways: through increased energy, detoxification, and external self-care. Much of what I've learned is from *Change Your Water . . . Change Your Life 2* by David Carpenter.

Increased Energy

One of the first things noticed when drinking enough ionized alkaline water is an increase in energy. When the day is done, *you're not*. What a change that is for most people—myself included.

Often when we say we don't have enough time, what we mean is that we don't have enough energy. The amount of energy people have is a direct reflection of the water they drink—the water's origin and organizational structure.

Carpenter states this: "The molecular geometry of structured water is very similar to the molecular geometry of crystalline quartz, based on the same pattern. This may be the reason that structured water is thought to carry signals more efficiently throughout living tissue. Many experts suspect that structured water may be the key to DNA signaling, enzyme activity, and many other functions. Structured water has also been shown to hydrate more effectively."

Detoxification

In today's world, we all carry the burden of toxic chemicals in our food and our environment. Many scientists believe these toxins are responsible for autoimmune diseases, mood disorders, chemical sensitivities, and a list of syndromes, among others. Many people have regained their health simply by reducing their toxic burden through drinking more water.

Our bodies are always working hard to eliminate toxins from our systems and at the same time keep our systems in a slightly alkaline state. The Standard American Diet is commonly referred to as the SAD diet simply because it's so very acidic. Our bodies store the excess toxins in fatty tissue, joints, and arteries, and eventually this buildup can kill you. It's seen in the continual rise in cancer, diabetes, heart disease, and obesity.

According to Carpenter, "Conditions that respond easiest to drinking ionized water are those linked with dehydration and/or acidosis. These include blood sugar problems, asthma and allergies, high blood pressure, skin problems, digestive and intestinal disorders, arthritis, and other joint problems." And about his patients who use alkaline, antioxidant, restructured water, he goes on to say, "These conditions often respond so quickly it surprises me."

External Self-Care

The ionizer makes alkaline water, but it also makes acid water, which has many uses externally. Our skin needs to be slightly acidic to do one of its jobs, which is protecting us from germs. The acid water with a pH between 4.5 and 5.5 is referred to as beauty water—it tightens, softens, and provides healing for common skin conditions, including nail fungus, rashes, psoriasis, acne, eczema, athlete's foot, cold sores, and diaper rash.

I've studied and continue to research water. I'm amazed at how interesting a subject it is and how much there is to learn. I would love it if everyone could change their lives! I believe that drinking and using the seven different kinds of water the best and most-awarded ionizer makes is the single most important change we all can make toward good health.

Change Your Water, Change Your Life

I'm excited to be a distributor of the finest high-technology water ionizer available and would love to provide it to you for your health and well-being. As part of my mission to increase consciousness in the world, I want to also increase our consciousness of the water we drink. You can order one of the various models of this ionizer or contact me at this website: www.4ConsciousWater.com.

CHAPTER 13

How to Be Conscious in an Unconscious World

Sometimes it feels like we're going around in circles. And we become discouraged when we seem to be back at the beginning again. Are you lost in the drama of life or *Maya*, as it's sometimes called?

I've asked that of myself when I notice I feel the world's suffering. It helps me notice I need to reconnect to Spirit, to God within, to remember who I really am. I wonder how I become lost in the illusions again and how to achieve the happiness I felt before as one with life.

If this sounds familiar, realize that the solution is a simple matter of getting back to the basics. We have the comfort of our daily spiritual practices.

A wise man, recognizing that the world is but

an illusion, does not act as if it is real,

so he escapes the suffering.

BUDDHA

Joseph Campbell, in his description of the hero's journey, explains that we indeed go through cycles. These cycles are separation and departure from the known, initiation by various trials and rites where true character emerges, and then the return in triumph to deserved recognition. This complete cycle then repeats in an ever-ascending spiral. There's no shame in starting over—it's all part of the journey upward. We are actually in a different place along the spiral than we were the last go-round.

Being Present Now

Many people spend their lives either reliving what has happened in their past or worrying about the future. We seem to find it difficult to stay present in the moment—with what's happening *now*. Yet the greatest gift we can give ourselves and others is to be present with them. This is called *quality time*. It's the connection we all long for but protect ourselves from fully merging with.

You may have heard the quote by Bil Keane, "Yesterday's the past, tomorrow's the future, but today is a gift. That's why it's called the present." The present is where our power is—the only place we can take action. This is the place where life really happens and where we create our reality. If we don't pay attention, life is over before we've really lived. Like Ralph Waldo Emerson said, "We are always getting ready to live, but never living."

In our earthly three-dimensional existence, there are only three possible time frames: past, present, and future. When you become conscious of your thoughts, you'll begin to become aware of how often your thoughts and feelings are focused on the past or in the future. As you become aware, call your attention back and return to the present.

It has been said that many people spend less than one percent of their time being fully present. The rest of the time is spent drifting in and out of "the *now*" as our attention wanders. Your mind may even seem to be out of your control. But with some consciousness and practice, you'll be able to be present more often. That's when you're *truly* living.

Living in the moment—also called *mindfulness*—is a state of active, open, intentional attention on the present. When you become mindful, you realize you're *not* your thoughts; you become an observer of your thoughts from moment to moment without judging them. The goal is to be fully engaged in your life experience.

Miranda Macpherson, one of my wonderful teachers, said "Do not abandon yourself." This statement made me realize that by not being mentally and emotionally present in my life, I was indeed abandoning myself and others. I vowed to do everything I could to be more present with my thoughts and feelings as they're happening.

Cultivating an awareness of the present bestows a host of benefits, such as a boost in immune functioning, reduction in chronic pain, lowering of blood pressure, and helping patients cope with fatal diseases. Spending time each day actively focusing on living in the moment reduces stress and thus alleviates one of the main causes of disease.

As we bring our awareness into the present moment, we become more conscious of our surroundings. We're then fully able to enjoy the beauty and messages of life that are found—the gift in every moment.

So why is it so hard to stay present? It's hard because many of the thoughts we have bring up feelings that make us extremely uncomfortable, taking us back to the past or projecting unwanted happenings into the future. Most people avoid being alone with their thoughts. It's amazing what people will do to avoid looking inward. They will do almost anything to be distracted from their inner self.

The basis for this fear of being present is usually that we believe something's wrong with us. We either look back and lament that we weren't "good enough" or we plan ahead, worrying about how we can do things "right" in the future. We're looking to be more perfect, win others' approval, or make sure nothing bad happens. This is an addictive habit.

> When I look back on all these worries,
> I remember the story of the old man
> who said on his deathbed that he had
> had a lot of trouble in his life, most
> of which had never happened.

WINSTON CHURCHILL

> People get so in the habit of worry that
> if you save them from drowning and put
> them on a bank to dry in the sun with
> hot chocolate and muffins they wonder
> whether they are catching a cold.

JOHN JAY CHAPMAN

The expert on the *now* is Eckhart Tolle, author of *The Power of Now*. My personal favorite of his books is *A New Earth: Awakening to Your Life's Purpose*. In an interview with Oprah Winfrey, Tolle explains several reasons to stay present:

- Recognize that the future has no reality but is only a thought form.
- Life consists entirely of the present moment.
- You can only think of the past or future in this moment.
- Be totally true to life by being present.

- Do your best in this moment.
- Life is only NOW!

GETTING BACK TO BASICS

No matter how much progress we make in awakening our consciousness, there will be times of starting over. Joseph Campbell explained it as the hero's journey cycle. Life is a series of beginning again. To facilitate this process of coming up to a higher vibration, what follows is a review of some things we've already covered:

- *Surrender again.* By that, I mean to stay in the present. Do your best and know that everything is always working out for you. Be in the flow of being guided and directed by Spirit.

- *Focus on what brings you joy.* Family, beauty, service, or whatever is in your experience that you love. Joy is our natural state of being, and God is love.

- *Express your gratitude.* Let people know you love them. Say thank-you to those who provide services for you, and connect with them visually and with a smile. Remind yourself of what you're grateful for right now—watch for things you may have overlooked.

- *Remember what's most important to you.* Refocus on what really matters, and "don't sweat the small stuff." Look at the big picture, and elevate yourself above the difficulties.

- *Connect directly to the Divine.* Say a prayer, meditate, call on an angel, get out in nature, sing praise to heaven—do anything that brings you closer to Source, whatever that means to you.

- *Use an affirmation that lifts you up from what's troubling you.* For example, say "I AM love in action,"

"I AM at peace with the way life unfolds for me," or "I know everything happens as it's meant for the greatest good." Repeat your affirmation until your brain accepts it as truth.

- *Make it interesting for yourself.* This process of reconnecting with higher consciousness will happen over and over again. Sometimes it feels as though you repeatedly start over—and it may become boring or feel like too much work. Try learning something new. There are many ways to enlightenment.

Remember the words of Lao Tzu: "There are many paths to enlightenment. Be sure to take one with a heart."

IT'S ALL GOOD, IF NOT PERFECT

Everything is perfect just the way it is. If God is everywhere and is the most powerful force in the universe, then creative intention assures us that everything is unfolding perfectly. It only seems otherwise when we aren't in tune with the energetic forces—our divine plan. But in truth, all is good. Everything that happens is designed to take us all closer to awakening and a higher consciousness.

The popular saying "It's all good" has its origin in rap music and ironically has now been adopted by the spiritual community. We close conversations with that saying to show acceptance for what has happened, inferring that everything is going to be okay. It means that every reversal is also an opportunity for personal growth.

With a perspective from higher consciousness, there are no mistakes or bad things happening. Everything is designed to invoke a step upward in consciousness. It's a new way of looking at life. Although it's sometimes difficult to embrace this kind of attitude when assailed with adversity, it's still possible and even necessary. As Tolle says, "Life will give you whatever experience is most helpful for the evolution of your consciousness. How do you know this is the experience you need? Because this is the experience you are having at the moment."

Accepting what happens in life requires a surrender of the ego's defensive personality that believes something's wrong. Nothing is wrong. It takes a disciplined mind to stop labeling every occurrence as good or bad and truly believe all is good. It just takes practice. In fact, by awakening, you become aware that life experience is all perfect just the way it is. Relax and enjoy the journey!

CHAPTER 14

WORLD SERVICE

As I entered my writing retreat in Colorado to complete this book, I set up my altar—a focus for meditation and prayer. I often use angel cards to get my messages for the day. I drew from my stack of Numerology Guidance Cards by Michelle Buchanan and got #99. This is an amazing number by itself—here it signifies compassion. One passage on the card was this: "Every time you feel someone else's pain as if it were your own, you raise your personal vibration and the vibration of the world." It's not easy to look at the pain of the world and feel the pain of those close to us. And more than ever before, we have access to world disasters of cataclysm and war via the Internet.

Sometimes I must remember that the pain I feel is not all my own. We often carry a part of world consciousness that needs to be lifted up. As an empath, it's always been difficult to feel all the pain around me. Now I can feel the energy and not turn away. I can breathe into it and begin to feel better.

Resist looking for trouble and for things to heal. The habit of trying to fix others is only accentuating their trials. The world is not broken but only going through growing pains. Know there will be opportunities that come to you to help you be all you *can* be. It is not your job to fix anything. Remember everything is unfolding perfectly.

This is a time of evolution for humanity. Many are living with wars, terrorist activities, the results of global warming trends, pollution of our planet, and cataclysms. To some, it's the fulfillment of the prophecy of the end of the world, a sign that extinction of the human race is within view. Others feel we're on the brink of a quantum leap forward in our evolutionary process. Which is it? Where do you stand with your talents, finances, and energetic attention in this equation? Which way do you vote when the energy is weighed?

Many organizations are springing up where you can participate in raising conscious awareness. Involve yourself in your interests. The opportunity is to engage with the world and with your life to live life consciously, which is my motto and on my website.

Conscious Evolution: Take Inspired Action

It's easy to see the news and become depressed about the world's situation and violence that hits too close to home. What can one person do? Awakening calls us to take inspired action. Futurist Barbara Marx Hubbard has given us some revolutionary answers in *Conscious Evolution: Awakening the Power of Our Social Potential*. Hubbard instructs us in the first steps:

> We work from within ourselves toward higher consciousness, greater freedom, and more complex order to affect a change in the world, first and foremost through our personal evolution.

The first way of accessing conscious evolution is to deliberately cultivate the capacity for inner knowing—"syntony"—spiritual resonance with the patterns of creation. We use our innate abilities to receive intuition, to act upon it, to accept feedback from the outside world . . . until we learn to act spontaneously and directly from whole-system intelligence.

Beyond that, we need to take action to survive. Hubbard further states, "[I]t is our responsibility to proactively design social systems that are in alignment with the tendency in nature toward higher consciousness, greater freedom, and more synergistic order."

I don't know about you, but I've been looking for a way to make a difference. I've been yearning to connect with like-minded people who are willing to make changes—in themselves, in their way of thinking, in their way of reacting, and in their way of showing up in the world. Many people are in embodiment already who can make a difference. Those who can and will make a difference are connecting.

People who "see the writing on the wall" and feel the pressure of energetic changes in the earth body know we're on the verge of birthing a new consciousness. As this happens, individually and as a species, let's focus on gathering together to co-create better designs for our social and economic systems.

> Real power to change happens
> when we connect
> what is working and empower one another to
> be the change we all want to see in the world.
>
> BARBARA MARX HUBBARD

The time has come, with advances in technology and the Internet as a communication network, to unite to create change. We can assist the world by accessing the best within us and linking to others who have the synergistic gifts to move us forward into a new age. If you want to connect to a global movement, visit the website of the Foundation for Conscious Evolution (see the Resources section). Join with like-minded people online and in your area.

If you have a passion, bring that forward and join with the best of what's working in America and the world. Engage in what Barbara Marx Hubbard describes on her website as the "quantum transformation as it unfolds, first in small groups to stabilize our higher consciousness and to affirm our higher qualities of being—evolutionary circles of all kinds to birth the universal human that each of us is."

Take a stand! This is a call to action. Even though you might not know how to contribute at this point, start down the path one step at a time and the next step will become clear.

Conscious Capitalism

Another organization I was introduced to is Conscious Capitalism. It is designed to be a way of thinking about capitalism and business that better reflects where we are now on the human journey to wholeness (see the Resources section for more information). Our consciousness strives to be a place where business is in touch with the state of our world today and fosters the potential of companies to make a positive impact.

The idea is to have conscious businesses that want to be galvanized by higher purposes that serve, align, and integrate the interests of all. Their higher state of consciousness makes visible to them the interdependencies that exist, allowing them to discover and harvest the synergies from opportunities that exist.

We are all looking to find conscious leaders who are driven by service to a company's larger purpose, all the people the business touches, and the planet we all share. Conscious businesses are those that want to have trusting, authentic, innovative, and caring cultures that make working with them a source of both personal growth and professional fulfillment. They also endeavor to create financial, intellectual, social, cultural, emotional, spiritual, physical, and ecological wealth for everyone involved.

Conscious businesses will help evolve our world so billions of people can flourish, leading lives infused with passion, purpose, love, and creativity—a world of freedom, harmony, prosperity, and compassion. Become involved where you can, knowing that the very best thing you can do for the world is to raise your own vibration and continue with your self-care.

CHAPTER 15

CONCLUSIONS AND INSIGHTS

As I look back over the past two years, my mind wants to measure how far I've come and quantify what's different. It has taken that long to be able to find my voice—both in writing and speaking. I've been impatient at times to be a new and completely changed person—to have all of life figured out.

It's important to me to come to a kind of closure at this point in the story, even though I know our journey is endless and eternal and the unfoldment of consciousness continues. This is just another chapter, and I would not want it any other way.

The angels tell me all the time to stop trying so hard and just relax. The fairies tell me to laugh, have fun, and go out in nature. My spirit guides reassure me that everything is working out for me. But I forget. It's not about doing anything, it's about how I'm being—whether I'm conscious and awakened about what already is. There are shifts on every level that I *can* acknowledge, which I share next.

Spiritual integration. Spirit has taken on a new dimension. There's a fullness in life and awe at the miracle of being. All the senses are alive with processing the energy flow. As I awaken, I feel closer to nature and the songs of the birds, and I can feel when the trees are swaying happily in the breeze. I feel the closeness of angels and fairies, as well as all the support of heavenly beings. I am more mindful and more soulful.

Life is about being, not doing. There's contentment in resting in a sense of being and knowing that everything is already complete in the *allness* of God. I practice breathing into situations knowing that the breath of consciousness will put me in contact with a higher-frequency vibration where I have access to answers that were not available to me before new vibrational perspective.

Emotional awareness. There's an awareness of how the energy flows in and through my system. I can feel subtle changes with the awareness of flickering thoughts and emotions that present themselves. I'm able, with intention and breath, to connect with Source energy and feel the buzz as the energy within amps up.

I feel the pain that others are experiencing the world over and hold them in my heart. At the same time, I'm protective of exposing myself to the energy patterns of those who are disruptive to my immediate force field. I notice there are some things I just don't need in my life anymore—they're no longer relevant. Disapproval and judgment from others doesn't sting now, and I'm also more available and supportive of family.

Mental patterns. The most important change here is the gradual disconnecting from the need to make judgments of others. When I have an understanding that we all have a path and a life story, I remember that these are a gift, an entryway, in awakening to oneness. I can only look on in amazement at the way people show up in their own lives. There's no need to be right, knowing everyone must go through his or her own experience to figure it all out—a knowing that everything works out for us all.

There's a quieting of the mind from the chatter that used to be present. A peacefulness now says I'm okay with the unknown. I'm happy to trust Source to flow through my life without pushing, pulling, and prodding. I rest in the space of just *being*.

Anchoring the light physically. A huge shift in my understanding is the realization that our call to action at this point in the evolution of humanity is to bring consciousness into the physical. Not only in our own understanding but into action in the world, and into the very space between the atoms of our cellular makeup. In the past, I used spirituality as an escape from dealing with the world, but no more.

There's a desire to contribute to the world in a meaningful way. Yet I need to be true to my highest self in how I take action and where. I ask myself the question, "What can I give from the heart?" But to give, I must support my physical body through the upgrade in energy vibration that's changing my very core. I've had to make changes in almost every area of my life to keep up with the vibratory spin on the planet, although that mostly means slowing down and being more deliberate. I no longer have interest in many of the things I used to do. Much has changed in the physical for sure.

Personal reflections. I find that I AM in love with the Divine. There's no feeling of being lonely since finding this new "love of my life." Love has been found, and I am profoundly held and supported. There's no more yearning and searching for completion, just a deepening. I notice I'm able to love more freely in my relationships.

The challenges of everyday life with family to take care of remain, but there's also a perspective that's not attached to an outcome. There's only the focus on the now and getting direction for the next step—and the next, and the next.

There's gratitude for all of life experience, yet there's a knowing that still so much more is yet to come. There's excitement and expectation connecting with and finding my "tribe"—the people with whom I resonate and want to experience more collaboration. And there's *you*, my readers, who can inspire me to an even larger self.

There's never an end—it's all about the journey. It's true what Abraham-Hicks says about life, "You cannot get it wrong. And you will never get it done."

FEELINGS ARE THE KEY

I'd known for many years about using positive thoughts and affirmations. Perhaps you saw the film *The Secret*. I became disillusioned by the film because it didn't seem to change anything for me. I followed Hicks and worked on "finding thoughts to feel better" but was still not able to manifest what I wanted. It only served to reinforce an idea that something was wrong with me.

Thanks to Mike Dooley, I found the missing ingredient—engaging the *feelings*! In other words, feeling happy, excited, victorious, and doing it as if it were already true. It seems that I could think the thoughts or say the words but not really let them into my emotional body. Remember that my emotional body was shut down, and I was afraid to feel my feelings. It takes some practice—and maybe some physical theatrical props—to get yourself into that emotionally energetic space.

Feelings are more than just emotion. Feelings are the movement of the energy vibration through your body. What I've learned to do is go for the energetic vibration of the feeling and anchor it into the physical body with movement—sing, jump up and down, dance, twist, breathe, and get the energy to flow. This may sound like splitting hairs, but it was a distinction that made all the difference to me. I suppose that's why indigenous tribes used singing and dancing in their ceremonies.

Once I learned to connect with my emotions, the feelings, and the energy vibrations, I could move through fear and give that needed creative power to my thoughts and affirmations. *That* understanding was what was lacking. Maybe this is an ingredient that's lacking in your creative visualization formula to manifest your dreams.

Most of us are very motivated by the desire to manifest our wants and wishes in the physical. The three-dimensional world seems more real and meaningful to us. But *things* are just representations of the feelings of happiness, of the wholeness we truly seek. Now I understand that it's the *feeling* we're striving for—that happiness, security, sense of accomplishment, or whatever it is that motivates us.

When we learn to go directly for a feeling, we don't really *need* the manifestation anymore. We can still go for all the physical things if we want them—but they're then just the next logical step, not the main event. When we already have integrated with the feeling, we set the energy pattern we were after in the first place. Make sense?

I didn't really get it until now. When you translate what I'm saying experientially, you'll understand what my words are pointing you toward. It took a long time for that understanding to click into place—for the key of feelings to open the lock of consciousness. Are you feeling excited yet? I know I am!

Awakening brings us the knowing that the energy— the *vibration*—is what's real, and everything we experience is a reflection in matter of that energy. It's these patterns that we translate, through our senses, into the world of form. Our understanding of reality shifts.

Awakening into this understanding, and the power of manifesting that comes with it, allows us to feel peace and reflect it into the world. We can embody the vibrational energy of love and transmute fear. As we all awaken to the wonder of full consciousness, the world, as a reflection of the energy vibration in us, will be made anew.

Many blessings for all that you are and in all that you do! May we all awaken in consciousness together and take our planetary home to the next dimension.

Afterword

Life has been unfolding for me as an ever-increasing blessing. While working on getting this book through the publishing process, synchronicity has brought my dreams toward me at an amazing rate. As I continue to connect to Source and stay in the flow with divinity through grounding myself and by anchoring the energetic changes in the physical body, my life experience is being totally transformed. There's no sign of depression anymore.

So much has happened in my life that's accelerating daily, and I'm excited to share it all in my next book. I've discovered the magic of sound therapy by using tuning forks to change the vibrations of the very cells in our body, thus allowing healing at every level of the four lower bodies that make up our individuated beings. I've connected with incredible people who support and love me as much as I love and wish to support them. I've found many exciting ways to make my awakening experience relevant to daily life.

Most important to me is the freeing of the energy that I'd tied up in my fears and the exhausting work of building and holding up my wall of invisibility. With the writing, publishing, and marketing of this book, I am outing myself as being a different "snowflake." It has been my intention throughout to just tell my story and speak my truth as it appeared to me. I want to encourage you to do the same.

It makes it safer for all of us to be who we are, to expand our consciousness, and to support others, as well as all life as it surrounds and supports us. It is my prayer that this book is of benefit to you as an individual, as I already know that this is of benefit to oneness as Consciousness itself.

BIBLIOGRAPHY OF RESOURCES

ARTICLES

Beliefnet. (n.d.). Ten Powerful Prayers for Healing and Change. Retrieved January 2017 from http://www.beliefnet.com/prayables/prayer-galleries/10-powerful-prayers-for-healing-and-change.aspx

Josh Clark. (n.d.). Can prayer heal people? *How Stuff Works: Health*. Retrieved January 2017 from http://health.howstuffworks.com/wellness/natural-medicine/alternative/prayer-healing.htm

Tiffany Gagnon. (n.d.). Men's Fitness: Diet Q&A: What It Means to Be Alkaline. Retrieved January 2017 from http://www.mensfitness.com/nutrition/what-to-eat/diet-qa-what-it-means-be-alkaline

Ronald Grisanti. (n.d.). Seven ways plastics damage the body. *Functional Medicine University*. Retrieved January 2017 from http://www.functionalmedicineuniversity.com/public/919.cfm

Harvard University Press. 2016. About This Book. Retrieved January 2017 from http://www.hup.harvard.edu/catalog.php?isbn=9780674064676

Knopf Doubleday Publishing Group. 2012. When God Talks Back by T. M. Luhrmann. Retrieved January 2017 from http://www.knopfdoubleday.com/2012/04/02/when-god-talks-back-by-t-m-luhrmann-2/

Mayo Clinic Staff. (n.d.). Water: How much should you drink every day? *Mayo Clinic*. Retrieved January 2017 from http://www.mayoclinic.org/healthy-lifestyle/ nutrition-and-healthy-eating/in-depth/water/art-20044256

Lee Standing Bear Moore. (n.d.). What does a spiritual awakening feel like? *Manataka American Indian Council*. Retrieved January 2017 from http://www.manataka.org/ page2632.html

Carl Llewellyn Weschcke. (n.d.). Microcosm and macrocosm. *Llewellyn Journal*. Retrieved January 2017 from https:// www.llewellyn.com/journal/article/2125

Robin Westin. 2015. Ten tips to cut your cancer risk. *AARP Magazine*. Retrieved January 2017 from http://www. aarp.org/health/healthy-living/info-2015/cancer-prevention-tips.html

Debra Williams. 1999. Scientific research of prayer: Can the power of prayer be proven? Retrieved January 2017 from http:// www.scienceforums.net/topic/42233-can-quantum-physics-one-day-explain-super-natural-phenomenon/

AUDIO PROGRAMS

Caroline Myss, *Channeling Grace: Invoking the Power of the Divine*. Available at http://www.soundstrue.com/store/ channeling-grace-4147.html

Shinzen Young, *The Science of Enlightenment: Teachings and Meditations for Awakening Through Self-Investigation*. Available at http://www.soundstrue.com/store/the-science-of-enlightenment-4027.html

BOOKS

Eben Alexander. 2012. *Proof of Heaven: A Neurosurgeon's Journey into the Afterlife*. New York, NY: Simon & Schuster.

John Beaulieu. 2010. *Human Tuning* Sound Healing with Tuning Forks. Stone Ridge, NY: BioSonic Enterprises Ltd.

Sarah Ban Breathnach. 1996. *The Simple Abundance Journal of Gratitude*. New York, NY: Warner Books.

Sarah Ban Breathnach. 2009. *Simple Abundance: A Daybook of Comfort and Joy*. New York, NY: Grand Central Publishing.

Candy Gunther Brown. 2012. *Testing Prayer: Science and Healing*. Cambridge, MA: Harvard University Press.

Joseph Campbell. 1949. *The Hero with a Thousand Faces*. New York, NY: Pantheon Books.

David Carpenter. 2014. *Change Your Water . . . Change Your Life 2*. Laguna Niguel, CA: YNR Marketing.

Mike Dooley. 2007. *Infinite Possibilities: The Art of Living Your Dreams*. New York, NY: Atria Books.

Masaru Emoto. 2005. *The Hidden Messages in Water*. New York, NY: Atria Books.

Eleanora Gilbert. 2011. *Conversations on Non-Duality: Twenty-Six Awakenings*. London, UK: Cherry Red Books.

Napoleon Hill. 2005. *Think and Grow Rich*. London, UK: Penguin.

Leonard G. Horowitz. 2011. *The Book of 528: Prosperity Key of Love*. Pahoa, HI: Medical Veritas International.

Barbara Marx Hubbard. 1998. *Conscious Evolution: Awakening the Power of Our Social Potential*. Novato, CA: New World Library.

Daniel Keyes. 2005. *Flowers for Algernon*. New York, NY: Mariner Books.

Jack Kornfield. 2001. *After the Ecstasy, the Laundry: How the Heart Grows Wise on the Spiritual Path*. New York, NY: Bantam Books.

CC Leigh. 2011. *Becoming Divinely Human: A Direct Path to Embodied Wakening*. Lafayette, CO: Wolfsong Press.

Bruce Lipton. 2008. *The Biology of Belief: Unleashing the Power of Consciousness, Matter and Miracles*. Carlsbad, CA: Hay House.

T. M. Luhrmann. 2012. *When God Talks Back: Understanding the American Evangelical Relationship with God*. New York, NY: Vintage.

Miranda McPherson, Joan Tollifson, and Vicki Woodyard. 2014. *The Journey Home: Discovering the Essential Self*. Dayton, OH: In the Garden Publishing.

Caroline Myss. 2013. *Archetypes: Who Are You?* Carlsbad, CA: Hay House.

Nick Ortner. 2014. *The Tapping Solution: A Revolutionary System for Stress-Free Living*. Carlsbad, CA: Hay House.

Rasha. 2006. *Oneness* (2nd ed.). Santa Fe, NM: Earthstar Press.

Teal Swan. 2016. *The Completion Process: The Practice of Putting Yourself Back Together Again*. Carlsbad, CA: Hay House.

Michael Singer. 2015. *The Surrender Experiment: My Journey into Life's Perfection*. New York, NY: Harmony.

Colin Tipping. 2010. *Radical Forgiveness: A Revolutionary Five-Stage Process to Heal Relationships, Let Go of Anger and Blame, and Find Peace in Any Situation*. Louisville, CO: Sounds True.

Eckhart Tolle. 2004. *The Power of Now: A Guide to Spiritual Enlightenment*. Vancouver, BC: Namaste Publishing.

Eckhart Tolle. 2008. *A New Earth: Awakening to Your Life's Purpose*. New York, NY: Penguin.

Neale Donald Walsch. 1998. *The Little Soul and the Sun*. Newburyport, MA: Hampton Roads Publishing.

Neale Donald Walsch. 2012. *The Only Thing That Matters*. London, UK: Hay House.

Ambika Wauters. 1997. *Chakras and Their Archetypes: Uniting Energy Awareness and Spiritual Growth*. Feasterville-Trevose, PA: Crossing Press.

HEALTH

ClearVite detoxification: https://www.apexenergetics.com/clearvite-family

Fat Flush Diet: http://fatflush.com

RepairVite program: http://drtracigiles.com/repairvite-program/

MISCELLANEOUS

Lisa Miller. 2014. *Discovering Heaven: How Our Ideas About the Afterlife Shape How We Live Today*. Special issue of *Time* (Summer)

Numerology Guidance Cards: http://www.
michellebuchanan.co.nz/numerology-oracle-cards/
Radical Forgiveness worksheet:
http://www.radicalforgiveness.com/free-tools/

MUSIC AND SOUND THERAPY

Music to Feel Better Song Sampler: http://www.
tupelokenyon.com
Oprah and Eckhart Tolle, Living in the Present Moment:
https://www.youtube.com/watch?v=KmCjR1_N14E
Power Thoughts Meditation Club (Solfeggio
Frequencies): https://www.youtube.com/user/
PowerThoughtsclub/about
The Supreme Heart of Shiva CD by Vidura Barrios
"Who Is the Watcher" by Tupelo Kenyon: https://www.
youtube.com/watch?v=PbsXGxl37Xk

WEB RESOURCES

Abraham-Hicks: https://www.youtube.com/user/
AbrahamHicks
Affirmations: http://www.louisehay.com/affirmations/
Conscious Capitalism: http://www.
consciouscapitalism.org/
Foundation for Conscious Evolution:
http://barbaramarxhubbard.com/
global-communication-hub-main/
Kangen Water: http://www.4ConsciousWater.com

WORKSHOPS & TRAINING

Miranda Macpherson, "Relaxing into God":
http://relaxingintogodcourse.com/
Mike Dooley, "Train the Trainer" Certification Course.
http://www.tut.com/Humanity

About the Author

LINDSAY S GODFREE is a contributing author in the number one best-selling 365 book series. Her articles are presented in the latest volume, *365 Life Shifts: Pivotal Moments That Changed Everything!*, published in February 2017. Lindsay is an "Infinite Possibilities: The Art of Changing Your Life" certified trainer. She is also a certified sound therapy technician. As creator of the Consciousness Guide website, Lindsay's passion is uplifting consciousness in every part of life. She lives in Apache Junction, Arizona, and has six beautiful daughters. Her interests include educating and inspiring others to live the life of their dreams, photography, and travel.

Please visit

<u>www.ConsciousnessGuide.com</u>
to learn more about Lindsay and her ongoing
trainings, sign up for her newsletter, and
join the Consciousness Community.

Printed in the United States
By Bookmasters